STILL-HUNTING
TROPHY
WHITETAILS

text and photographs by
Bill Vaznis

STACKPOLE
BOOKS

0 11557 03419 6

Copyright © 2007 by Bill Vaznis

Published by
STACKPOLE BOOKS
5067 Ritter Road
Mechanicsburg, PA 17055
www.stackpolebooks.com

Printed in China

First edition

10 9 8 7 6 5 4 3 2 1

Cover design by Wendy Reynolds
Cover photograph by Bill Vaznis

Library of Congress Cataloging-in-Publication Data
Vaznis, Bill.
    Still-hunting trophy whitetails / Bill Vaznis. — 1st ed.
        p. cm.
    Includes index.
    ISBN-13: 978-0-8117-3419-6
    ISBN-10: 0-8117-3419-6
    1. White-tailed deer hunting. 2. Still hunting. I. Title.

SK301.V39 2007
799.2'7652—dc22
                                                                2006038364

Contents

Introduction   v

PART I: An Introduction to Still-Hunting
1   Six Silent Steps   3
2   Still-Hunting Myths   13
3   Basic Equipment   24
4   How to Play the Wind   35
5   Sounds of Silence   44
6   How to Beat Buck Fever   51

PART II: Successful Still-Hunting Strategies
7   Cutting Corners: Still-Hunting New Property   63
8   The Plan   73
9   Calling on the Prowl   82
10   How to Still-Hunt a Bedding Area   91
11   Walking the Line   100
12   Still-Hunting the Peak of the Rut   108

PART III: Still-Hunting Tactics for Bowhunters
13   Advanced Bowhunting Skills   123
14   The Moment of Truth   133
15   Bowhunting Thin Cover   139
16   After the Shot   145
17   Lessons Learned   155
18   Thirty Hours with a Boone & Crockett Buck   165

PART IV: Still-Hunting with Firearms
19   How to Wear Blaze Orange Effectively   175
20   The Connection is Clear-Cut   184
21   Stalking Bucks on Thunder Road   196

22   Are You Sure You Missed?   205

23   Blood-Trailing Marginally Hit Bucks   213

24   Shooting Tips That Will Save Your Season   220

25   First Blast!   233

Index   241

Introduction

nthropologists tell us that primitive man evolved in part because of his abilities to still-hunt big game animals. I don't doubt that for a minute. Hunger is a great motivator! Today, however, still-hunting is the most difficult and least understood method of tagging any animal—especially a whitetail buck. Why? Put simply, we appear to have lost our natural ability to sneak about the forest undetected.

For many outdoorsmen, the term still-hunting seems to be a contradiction in terms, but whoever coined the term knew exactly what he was talking about. Still-hunting is not "standing still" in a tree stand, "sitting still" in a ground blind, or "posting" for unseen drivers. No, a true still-hunter does not wait in ambush for a shot but rather actively pursues his quarry on foot. Alone, he challenges the buck's eyes, ears, and nose by sharing the same terrain, ground cover, and wind currents as his adversary.

To get close enough to a buck for a shot, a still-hunter must learn to move with the rhythms of nature, much like ancient man. Once mesmerized by this rhythm, a still-hunter is no longer a passive observer but rather an active participant in the scheme of things. He becomes what nature has always intended him to be—a true predator.

WHY STILL-HUNT?

The conversation around the campfire was innocent enough, until it centered on ambushing whitetails from a treestand. My friend chastised me for no longer hunting out of a portable platform, electing instead to sneak about Indian style for my venison. Why, he asked me rather impertinently, would anyone want to make the sport even more difficult than it already is by still-hunting? In fact, he added, why would anyone not want to take advantage of all the modern advancements in archery? This would, he argued, lower the number of misses, lower the number of poorly hit animals, and increase success rates—making treestand hunters better all-around deer hunters.

The author with a nice nine-point buck taken while still-hunting.

"Hogwash," I said to him, and in no uncertain terms, told him why. You erect a treestand high into a copse of trees, I told him, or weave it into a tangle of branches, in an effort not to be seen. You will then trim away troublesome branches to make raising your rifle or coming to full draw easier, and will at times even add branches or bolts of camo cloth to your stand to further conceal your position. Your goal is to completely hide your human form from a buck's prying eyes.

Then you clean the tree of shards of bark and do whatever is necessary to stop the squeaks and groans that are inherently present in the treestand, including coating the chains with plastic and adding carpeting to the platform. Your goal is to completely eliminate all manmade sounds from a buck's radar-like ears.

Of course, I added, you position yourself high enough into the branches so that if the wind does change, an errant puff of human stench will pass harmlessly above a buck's nose. Your goal is to completely eliminate human odor from the equation.

What have you accomplished? You have not made yourself a better hunter or a better woodsman, I argued. In fact, you have done just the opposite. Instead of challenging a buck's senses, you have worked at eliminating the very qualities that make him special. Indeed, you may as well put blinders on the buck's eyes because it is unlikely he will ever see you hiding twenty or thirty feet above him. And while you are at it, you may as well stuff cotton in his ears and swab Vaseline in his nose because it also unlikely he will ever hear you or smell you, either. You may as well put a treestand up in a pasture and shoot a cow because you have reduced the finest game animal in North America to that of a common barnyard animal.

And why on earth, I asked my friend, would a true hunter want that to happen?

PART I
An Introduction to Still-Hunting

Six Silent Steps

L et's get right down to brass tacks. Still-hunting whitetail deer is never easy. For starters, our primary senses are dull by comparison to a mature buck, and we spend precious little time in the outdoors honing them. Our eyes are glued to television sets, our ears to iPods and other music devices, and our noses—well, we spend a fortune each year disguising odors that offend our delicate nostrils. It is no wonder deer easily sidestep our approach; we are no longer wild creatures of the forest!

As a society we are also consumed by the need to take shortcuts with up-to-date technology. Archery magazines are full of ads promising instant success in the deer woods with page after page of gimmicks and sure-fire doodads that guarantee us a clean shot at a trophy buck. Although a few of these advances, like GPS systems and deer calls, do allow us to spend more time in the deer woods and can actually enhance our hunting experience, most of these gadgets only serve to mask our inadequacies. Do we really need arrow shafts that talk to us when lost?

So just how does a still-hunter put the sneak on a buck today? With luck

If you want to bow-bag a buck by still-hunting, then you need to get close—really close!

some would say, but over the years I've tagged twenty-odd whitetails "sneaking and peeking" with archery tackle. All it takes is practice—and the determination to follow these six steps.

1. HIDE IN PLAIN SIGHT

The first step is complete camouflage. A whitetail has an incredible sense of vision that's geared towards picking up motion. You wave a bare hand, for example, and a deer will spot it—even from a great distance. Thus, you need to camouflage not only your entire body, including any exposed skin, but all your equipment, too. You can't be too careful in this regard. Wave a shiny bow about loaded with a full quiver of brightly fletched arrows, and a whitetail buck will certainly take notice!

And speaking of quivers, leave the hip-style arrow quiver home. Try this exercise and you will see why. Have a buddy walk past your line of vision with a hip quiver attached to his belt, and you will readily see that with each step the fletching waves back and forth like a handful of brightly colored handkerchiefs.

Of course, the quiver is not the only piece of equipment with which you need to be concerned. Too many of today's bows are designed by Madison Avenue executives to catch your eye—bright and shiny sells! If need be, I spray-paint my bow with dull earth tones, paying close attention to any white

Pay attention to detail and try to camouflage yourself and your equipment thoroughly.

lettering on the limbs and any shiny nuts, bolts, and washers. I shy away from jewelry, especially fancy belt buckles and gold necklaces, and elect to tuck my watch up under my sleeve. If you wear glasses, stay away from silver and gold frames and wear a pair made from dark plastic instead.

I then smear washable camo cream war paint on my face, neck, ears, and eyelids before I step afield. A man's bright face is a danger signal understood by nearly every mature whitetail, and one glimpse is all it takes to send an unseen buck hi-tailing over the nearest ridge. Unless you can only hunt an hour or so before work and need to keep your face clean to keep your job, stay away from head nets and facemasks as they tend to obscure your vision, muffle sounds, and deflect subtle changes in wind direction.

Finally, don't be afraid to mix and match different camouflage designs from various manufacturers. They sometimes break up the human figure far better than a single-design outfit. The rule of thumb here is to wear a cap and jacket that match what is growing above ground and pants that match what is laying on the ground. For example, a gray-based jacket and brown leaf-style pants are a dynamite combination for sneaking through the beech trees after leaf drop. Keep in mind that any homemade pattern that distorts a hunter's outline out to 35 yards or so has a lot going for it, with large blotches of starkly contrasting colors more effective at hiding movements than pants and jackets with many threat-like squiggles.

2. LEARN THE LAY OF THE LAND

Your next step towards better still-hunting is learning your hunting territory like the back of your hand. Aerial surveys, typographical maps, and shoe leather will soon get you on intimate terms with your whitetail hotspot. Start out by following logging roads, power lines, and streambeds to get a general feel for the terrain. Then get off the beaten path.

Carry your topographical maps with you and study them in the field. Locate and examine those features that appear to promote deer travel, such as natural bottlenecks, ridges, saddles, steep or gradual slopes, swamps, or large bodies of water. Look for tracks, deer runs, and buck rubs to verify your suspicions.

It's also important to locate natural food sources like abandoned apple orchards and grown-over clear-cuts in the big woods, and manmade food supplies like corn, wheat, and alfalfa in farm country. Check out these food sources during the early morning and late evening hours to learn the direction of prevailing winds and then walk the edges to discover preferred entrance and exit trails. Backtrack some of these trails to locate probable bedding areas.

Notice the numerous ways whitetails take full advantage of typographical features, air currents, and available cover to travel undetected from

A topographical map is the Bible of the ardent still-hunter. But like the Good Book, it is of little value if you don't take the time to read it.

bedding area to feeding area. This information will help you later on with scent control, and as the rut unfolds, it will often dictate your rate of speed and course of travel, too.

3. CONTROL YOUR SCENT
Knowing the lay of the land and the whereabouts of bedding areas, travel corridors, and preferred food sources will help you deal more effectively with a whitetail's incredible sense of smell. How? You will no longer be spreading your human scent to the four winds as you wander aimlessly about the woods in search of a hat-rack buck. Rather, you will be confidently pussyfooting downwind or crosswind of known concentrations of deer.

Nonetheless, don't expect a masking scent to cover any extended downwind travel. I use real skunk juice to momentarily confuse a buck if the wind suddenly changes direction or if I find myself in the delightful predicament of being 20 yards and crosswind from a buck headed into the wind. I never depend on any masking scent to get me within bow range of any downwind whitetail, however.

Human scent that is carried away with a breeze soon dissipates and is then no longer a threat. I'm more concerned with the scent I leave behind on the ground. It can linger long enough to spook a nice buck out of the area long after I've left the scene. Indeed, once a buck knows you are sneaking around his bailiwick, he will react by changing his travel routes, and he may alter his feeding and bedding schedules, too. He may even go nocturnal.

I learned how quickly a dirty scent trail can spook a buck early in my bowhunting career when a 130-class buck about turned himself inside out after bumping into my entrance trail. He couldn't wait to escape the stench and vamoosed into the nearest wood-lot, never to be seen again. Now I wear knee-high rubber boots religiously, often dousing them with fox or coyote urine for added protection.

4. DETERMINE YOUR SPEED

It is a well-known fact that a buck's eyes are geared towards detecting movement, and any movement, no matter how slight, can send a smart buck hi-tailing it over the nearest ridge. Given this fact, at what speed should a still-hunter slip through the woods? Is a half-mile an hour too fast? How about 100 yards an hour? Is this still too fast? What about 10 yards in 10 minutes? Is it possible for a still-hunter to go too slow?

Never depend on masking scents, urines, or chemical deodorizers to get you within bow range of any downwind whitetail.

Well, your chances of catching a buck flatfooted are really governed by more than speed. You see, there are times when a still-hunter should be traveling right along through the woods, even working up a sweat. There are other times, however, when a still-hunter should be grateful for the time he has and move no more than a foot or so a minute—with all his senses alert and wired tight for immediate action!

How do you know when to speed up? How do you know when to drop it in low gear and just creep forward? Well, that depends on a number of factors. Let's take a closer look at the more important ones.

Sign Under Foot

There is no use still-hunting along a creek bottom or along the edge of a field if there is no fresh deer sign nearby. In fact, nothing will ruin a future still-hunter faster than to spend the day crawling through the woods at a snail's pace and not see a deer. You have got to still-hunt places deer habitually frequent if you expect to fill a tag.

If all you are seeing are flags, then you are probably still-hunting too fast for current conditions.

Sometimes, however, still-hunters want to check out an abandoned orchard or a hardwood ridge above a clear-cut for deer and deer sign. Under these circumstances, there is no use scouting in slow motion, even if the season is open. I walk right along while looking for tracks, rubs, scrapes—and deer. If I come upon fresh sign, I will immediately slow down to first assess the situation and then to study the terrain for more evidence of deer.

Time of Day

Even if there is plenty of sign underfoot, that does not mean you should immediately begin slipping in and out of the shadows looking for deer. There may be a plethora of tracks and rubs along the edge of a cut cornfield, for example, but it would be folly for you to still-hunt here at high noon early in the season. The chances of you happening upon a buck then are nil. It would be just as foolish for you to skip past a known bedding area late in the evening. Going too fast then will surely lessen your chances of a sighting.

One of the goals of a still-hunter is to be in the right place at the right time. This means studying deer sign, the lay of land, the wind, and a host of other factors before committing yourself to being at a specific locale at a certain time. You might, for instance, want to sneak through the brush adjacent to the cornfield at first light and then slip silently along the edge of the bedding area later in the day at dusk.

Stage of the Rut

Of course, if the rut is in full swing, sneaking along the edge of a feeding area known to be frequented by family groups of does and fawns might be a good tactic at any time of the day. Bucks are on the prowl now all day long in search of an estrous doe. And one of the places they keep coming back to is a choice feeding area preferred by does.

Still-hunting slowly along the edge of a buck's bedroom when he is more likely to be out chasing the girls is not likely to produce much action—unless, of course, the thicket you are cruising is also home to a herd of does and fawns!

Ground Conditions

Nothing slows a still-hunter down faster than crunchy leaves or dry, brittle branches littering the forest floor. You have several options when ground conditions are not optimal.

The first is to choose a different route. Maybe there is a cart road nearby or a fencerow that can offer you quiet

One of the goals of a still-hunter is to be in the right place at the right time, and that means taking several factors into account before you step afield.

passage. You can also wait until it rains or until the sun melts the morning frost, thus dampening the forest debris. Or you can abandon the area until ground conditions are more favorable. Indeed, the only time to still-hunt a particular route is when all the conditions are in your favor. Otherwise, you risk spooking the buck and making him more wary of your presence.

Finally, you can take the debris-riddled route, but plan on only sneaking forward during prime time at 10 yards an hour. And you better make it good because you will probably only get away with it once.

Wind

Storm fronts are good days to be afield in part because the howling winds, rustling leaves, and swaying vegetation tend to mask your forward progress, which allows you to sneak around at a bit faster pace than you normally would. Indeed, you are less likely to be seen, heard, or scented during stormy weather.

As you can see, there is no steadfast rule governing a still-hunter's forward progress. At prime time in a prime location on a rainy, windy afternoon during the peak of the rut, I might still-hunt so slowly grass will seem to grow underfoot. But if this hotspot is on the far side of the hill, I might just jog through the hardwoods to get there!

Butane lighters, a feather attached to your bow, and a wet finger can all indicate wind direction. With practice, you can accurately detect subtle variations in direction or wind speed by simply paying attention to ground-hugging vegetation and the wind on exposed skin.

5. CONTROL YOUR NOISE

Bowhunters who traditionally hunt from elevated platforms often think it is folly to still-hunt for whitetails. They erroneously believe that for still-hunters to be successful, they must slip through dry leaves and crackling underbrush without ever making a sound. Nothing could be further from the truth. I've tagged several bucks while still-hunting in dry leaves, including a 140-class nine-pointer I caught one frosty morning working a scrape line.

The next time you are in the deer woods, close your eyes and listen to the forest din. Feeding, playing, traveling, and spooked animals all make lots of noise. When I'm still-hunting, I prefer to imitate the muted footsteps of a feeding whitetail. Their tempo, rhythm, and speed suit me just fine. If I stumble or make any alarming sounds, I'll blow a few short notes from my fawn call. Fawns are a noisy lot in the deer woods, and that bleat will often relax any nearby deer.

Of course, unnatural sounds are to be avoided. A few seasons back I caught a mature eight-pointer flatfooted in a grown-over cut. I thought he was going to be an easy kill, and at 10 yards he should have been, but I failed to snap my nock onto the string with finesse. That buck heard the soft plastic slip over the string and vamoosed in a flash. I never did see him again.

Brush slapping against your outer clothing can also send a buck into hiding. Get into the habit of wearing only wool or washed cotton, as both are quiet. When temperatures dip to the single digits, however, it's tough to beat wool.

Finally, your calf-high rubber boots should be equipped with Air Bob soles. They will help you maintain your balance over rough and uneven terrain, allowing you to "sneak and peek" with ease and quiet determination. As an added bonus, you'll be surprised how warm your feet stay on an icy November morning.

6. SEE HIM FIRST

The cornerstone to tagging a buck is seeing him before he sees you, which is not always an easy task in the deep woods, swamps, and abandoned farmlands he calls home. And the practice is made more difficult by the manner in which we hunters usually walk—we like to constantly watch where our feet are going! The real trick to still-hunting is learning to move forward with your eyes glued to the cover ahead—not on the ground. Your eyes must be searching for a buck full time.

In prime habitat, your forward progress should be undertaken in a slow and deliberate manner. Look down briefly to locate a safe, quiet passageway. Then, as you continue to scan for bucks, take one or two steps without looking down. You will suddenly discover a whole new vista to examine, so take

To get the drop on a fat buck, learn to imitate the muted steps of a feeding whitetail.

your time using your binoculars to probe the shadows and edge habitat for unusual shapes and out-of-context colors. Only after you are sure there are no bucks in the area should you search about on the ground for deer sign.

To do your searching, leave the minis home and elect to use a mid-sized quality pair of optics. Nikon, Burris, Leica, Swarovski, and Zeiss immediately come to mind. They are waterproof, soundproof, and easy on the eyes after a day afield.

Once these still-hunting movements are mastered, your presence in the deer woods will no longer be recognized as that of an alien intruder—a series of steps equidistant in time and space and predictable in direction of travel—but rather as a natural member of the forest community. Primitive man did it and so did North America's first natives. With practice, so can you!

Still-Hunting Myths 2

The arrow struck with a resounding W-H-A-C-K, nearly knocking the eight-pointer off his feet. I waited a half-hour, or close to it, and took up the blood trail, finding the buck piled up about 100 yards distant. Still-hunting along a scrape line at first light certainly paid off for me that day.

Later, back at camp, a friend helped me hang my buck in the shade. "Why on earth do you like still-hunting for whitetail deer so much?" he asked me as we hoisted the buck off the ground. "I can't even walk to my treestand without spooking a deer. You're either part Indian or just plain lucky!"

Well, my grandmother's grandmother was an Indian, but that's not why I like to still-hunt, or why I rarely go a season anymore without filling a tag. Still-hunting is a demanding and frustrating hunting method, but it's also the most rewarding.

Why then don't more bowhunters try still-hunting? Brainwashing! The old salts of the hunting fraternity tell us still-hunting deer with a bow and arrow is an impossible task, so we dumbly believe them. Well, here are the reasons they often give, and the real

Too many bowhunters have been brainwashed into thinking that still-hunting whitetails with archery tackle is a waste of time. What a shame! Nothing is more rewarding than taking a buck Indian-style!

13

facts of the matter. Keep in mind that ancient man still-hunted for hundreds of thousands of years before the portable treestand was mass-marketed to the modern bowhunter.

MYTH: You won't see as many deer if you choose to still-hunt.
FACT: The fact of the matter is you'll see more!

If you sit in a treestand or a ground blind along the periphery of a swamp, you may see one or two of the deer that are known to frequent the area. You are limited, of course, by the distance you can see from your stand. A still-hunter, on the other hand, will sneak along a quarter- or half-mile of that same swamp and possibly see as many as ten of the deer that use the edge as a travel route simply because he is covering more ground during prime time.

It's much like riding the back roads in July while looking for deer. If you just sit and glass one field, you might see a dozen whitetails emerge as dusk approaches. If you drive from field to field, however, you could see two or three dozen deer because you are checking out more territory during that same 90 minutes. Of course, you won't get that kind of mileage still-hunting, but the principle is the same.

It is an indisputable fact: still-hunters see more deer than treestand hunters.

A second reason still-hunters see more deer is they have a better idea where to look. Some of the parcels I have hunted over the years are a second home to me. Drop me off at midnight, and I'll tell you exactly where I am without the aid of a map or a flashlight. Since still-hunters cover more ground on a regular basis, it is inevitable that they will better understand the nuances of deer travel in that region and thus know more good places to look for deer.

Still-hunters can react immediately to changes in the deer woods, whereas it might take a week for the treestand hunter to realize the deer are feeding elsewhere.

This leads us to the third reason still-hunters see more deer: in-season scouting. Stand hunters routinely stay out of most of a buck's bailiwick, electing to sneak in and out of their treestands with a minimum of disturbance. However, changes in food preferences, human pressure, and the rut can all have a deleterious effect on the best of treestand locations. In fact, it could take a stand hunter days or even a whole season to realize what changes have occurred and how to best react to them.

But a still-hunter spends every day he hunts looking for deer and deer sign and can react immediately to any change in hunting conditions. He knows, for example, that last night's windstorm may have knocked a thousand sweet acorns to the ground. He will forgo hunting the apple orchard for a few days to check it out. A still-hunter knows the farmer harvested his corn this morning, and the deer won't be using the adjacent draw as a conduit any longer. He'll be poking around the wooded hillside for the next few days instead. A still-hunter knows there is an illegal treestand 300 yards up the hill from yours, and this hunter has been intercepting "your" deer. A still-hunter will avoid the area. And a still-hunter knows there is a fresh scrape line on the far side of the swamp; a scrape line no one else knows about. He'll be sneaking and peeking along that scrape line when the buck returns in the morning while the two treestand hunters battle it out on the near side.

Finally, still-hunters see more deer than stand hunters because they are not as dependent on the weather, a steady wind, or the natural movements of deer for a sighting. If the weather turns sour and the deer hole up for a few days, a treestand hunter will be hard pressed to see a buck. But a still-hunter can hunt the lee side of hills or put the sneak on bedded deer during that same period of inclement weather and have plenty of action.

You don't have to be deathly quiet to still-hunt successfully. It is the kind of noise you make that makes the difference.

If the wind changes direction at prime time, a still-hunter simply rolls with the punches and changes course, too. But a stand hunter must abandon the site or risk being detected. Either way, the evening is probably lost for him.

And finally, a still-hunter can slip through an orchard and catch a buck feeding at dusk while a treestand hunter sits helplessly in the wrong stand 100 yards distant waiting anxiously for that same buck to enter a nearby alfalfa lot during legal shooting hours.

MYTH: To still-hunt successfully, you can't make any noise.
FACT: You can get away with making all kinds of noise, if you learn how. Rhythm and tempo are the keys.

Have you ever sat in your treestand and wondered if the rustling you hear in the leaves behind you is a squirrel or a buck? It's sometimes difficult to tell the difference, in part because there is no prolonged and predictable sequence to each series of footfalls.

Next time you have the opportunity to watch a deer feed, make note of its footsteps. Unlike man, the cadence is not characterized by a purposeful gait. In other words, the steps are not equidistant and unidirectional in nature. The rhythm of a man walking and a deer feeding is as different as a waltz is to a foxtrot.

When I'm still-hunting, I want to be as quiet as a mouse, but if there are dry leaves about, I like to mimic the muted sounds of a feeding deer. I can get away with scuffing a few leaves now and then, and the speed is perfect for catching a buck in a relaxed state.

If you snap a twig while still-hunting, so what! Fawns make a tremendous amount of noise in the woods when they play. So do bucks when they chase does around during the breeding season. If you make an unwanted noise, just stop for a few seconds and blow on a grunt tube. A fawn bleat works all the time, but a couple of three-second buck "errrrps" during the peak of the rut may bring a nearby buck right to you in search of that fawn or hot doe you are "tending," with your clumsiness acting as an integral part of the charade!

MYTH: You can fool a buck's nose with a good cover-up scent. And its corollary: deer lures don't work.
FACT: Wrong and wrong.

It's been said that a whitetail's sniffer is 300 to 1,000 times better than a human's. You won't get any argument here. I have tried all kinds of cover-up scents on deer, and all were to no avail. Yes, you can shower regularly and wear only clean clothing stored in plastic bags stuffed with dirt, twigs, dead leaves, and the like, and you will reduce the amount of human scent in the air, but eventually he will get a whiff of you through all the dirt and dead-leaf smelling clothing. You can reduce human odor, but you can't eliminate it entirely.

Ground odors are more damaging that airborne odors simply because they can alert a deer to your presence hours after you have gone home.

Hot strategy: still-hunt 20 or 30 yards downwind of a scent trail.

I'm more concerned with the scent I leave on the ground after I pass by. Airborne odors quickly disappear with the first breezes, but ground odors can linger for hours, giving a buck the knowledge you are working the area long after you've gone home.

I'm very careful what I brush up against, and I always wear rubber boots, with fox urine sometimes squirted to an attached scent pad. Even then I do not still-hunt the same piece of real estate more than once or twice a week for fear of alerting area deer and thus causing them to change their daily routines.

Do lures work? Try this for yourself, and then you tell me. Take your favorite doe-in-heat lure, and once the rut is underway, lay a scent trail downwind of a doe's preferred bedding area. Do this by slowly still-hunting crosswind as close to the bedding area as possible without actually entering it. If you try this in the early morning after a cold front has passed, keep especially alert because you may run head-on into a buck as you are laying down the trail (hint!).

Now, turn about and still-hunt back along that same trail, only this time stay 20 or 30 yards downwind. Bucks scent-checking that bedding area for estrous does will generally do so by first working the downwind edges. If one picks up your scent trail, he will be coming broadside to you with his nose to the ground, giving you ample time to pick a spot, draw, aim, and shoot.

Other good strategies for scent trails include feeding areas frequented by does and rub lines that connect one doe bedding area with another. Just keep in mind that you are tracing the path a rutting buck takes as he patrols his bailiwick in search of estrous does and you'll see action.

MYTH: Because you have to move so slowly while still-hunting, it's boring!
FACT: There's a time to go slow and there's a time to move fast.

But boring? Just wait until you catch the "how-the-hell-did-you-get-so-close?" look on a buck's face; it's a natural high!

Still-hunters can get understandably frustrated when they believe they must sneak about at a snail's pace all day long. But to move slowly through areas devoid of deer, at a time of day when deer are not likely to be present, or in opposition to the rut, makes no more sense than sitting in a treestand in mid-August overlooking an open food plot at high noon!

The time to sneak and peek is when you expect to see a deer at any moment. When I'm still-hunting through an abandoned field late in the afternoon, for example, I'm often moving less than two feet per minute because I know bucks will often linger in this field before exposing themselves to feed in a nearby alfalfa lot after dark. I'll slip around that same field in a New York minute, however, to get to an adjacent bedding area on a windy afternoon.

MYTH: The best hunting strategy is to take a stand early and late in the day, and then still-hunt around noon.
FACT: The best time to still-hunt is early and late in the day—when the deer are moving—and all day during the rut!

The best time to still-hunt is when the deer are up and about. In the early season, mornings and evenings produce the most sightings as deer travel between feeding and bedding areas in a predictable manner. As the rut approaches, however, the action switches to rub lines and scrape lines with morning action lasting until almost noontime. When the rut peaks, you'll want to hunt all day because bucks will be continuously on the move then in search of an estrous doe.

The point is—why would you want to still-hunt when your chances are less than good? You want to capitalize on deer movement by still-hunting when the deer are on the move.

SCRAPE LINE MAGIC

The ravine reeked of big-buck sign. I had stumbled upon the ancient creek bed late that afternoon and was impressed with the amount of deer sign it hid from local eyes. Several thigh-sized rubs dotted the edge of the ravine like lighthouses in the fading light, but what interested me most was a fresh scrape line that ran along the rim for a bit before dipping down into the basin. Several scrapes had over-hanging licking branches the diameter of my grunt tube, and the nearby soft earth was littered with large splayed tracks.

There were also a half-dozen or more doe runs that passed through the ravine and up the far side, where the does apparently hid out during daylight hours. These doe runs intersected the scrape line at right angles, and the scrapes positioned at each juncture had been freshened on a regular basis.

"It's an ideal setup," I told my friend Judd Cooney back at camp that evening, "and with any luck I'll at least catch a glimpse of that buck working the scrape line at first light. I'm sure he's a wall-hanger!"

I had trouble sleeping that night in anticipation of what the morning could bring. I was up and at 'em well before first light, and I quickly grabbed a Danish and gulped down a cup of hot coffee before driving to within a half-mile of the ravine in my 4×4. The stars were still shining bright as I slipped through the woods to the old cart road that led to the head of the ravine. There I waited for shooting light to filter through the early-morning cloud cover before dropping down into the basin. The excitement was killing me.

It had been a long night for the buck, too. He had spent the darkest hours cruis-ing the cut corn lot to the north and then zigzagging through the series of hay mow-ings that lay between the big woodlot and the open river. He crossed the water back and forth several times where the shallows rippled over fallen leaves before cutting back to the big woodlot just as pink light was stirring in the east.

There were other bucks sniffing around, too, but most of the does had been bred and the pickings were getting lean. Gaunt now from the rigors of the rut and weighing just 200 or so pounds on the hoof, the nine-pointer passed along the downwind edge of the lot before circling back through a gold-enrod field where does were known to bed. He rousted two from the briars, but they were no longer in estrus and he quickly lost interest.

This rub was a tip-off that a good buck was working the area.

He turned again and trotted across an open pasture that bordered a steep ravine. A series of scrapes here bisected several doe trails that led from the nearby cornfields to a brushy hillside the does were indeed using as a daytime refuge. He was familiar with the ravine and wasted no time scent-checking each scrape as the morning's first light filtered through the cloud cover.

A heavy frost had coated the oak leaves and each step the buck took crackled along the ravine like a firecracker on the Fourth of July. I immediately recognized the cadence, even from deep down in the ravine, and my heart began to pound. I craned my neck back and forth along the top of the ravine until I caught the tips of the buck's tall rack weaving and bobbing along the rim. He was upon me in seconds and would soon pass out of range, so I quickly nocked a broadhead without taking my eyes off that rack, but I still could not see enough of the deer to take a clean shot.

The right place at the right time—and a perfect shot.

Suddenly, providence smiled on me and the 140-class buck stepped out to the edge to peer down into the ravine. The angle was steep, maybe 60 degrees, but I split my two pins and held solid for 30 yards for a long second before releasing a razor-tipped aluminum shaft at his vitals.

The arrow hit with a resounding W-H-A-C-K, as if someone had hit a nearby oak with a green 2×4. The buck suddenly lurched forward at the shot, ducked under an overhanging branch, and disappeared from sight in seconds. Then all was quiet. I peered along the bottom of the ravine for the escaping buck but saw nothing. I marked my shooting location but couldn't get the whacking sound out of my head, so after a long 20-minute wait, I climbed to the top of the ravine wondering if my shaft had not gone low, striking that huge oak on the far side of the deer.

But that was not the case. I found my blood-soaked arrow at the base of the oak and a blood-splattered trail that eventually led to the Pope & Young buck some 100 yards distant. The shaft had entered the buck low and just behind the near leg. With near surgical precision, it passed through the lungs, breaking the far leg upon exiting. The three-and-a-half-year-old buck never knew what hit him.

After field-dressing the buck, I realized a matching tenth point would have tallied the rack in the mid-150s, but I didn't care. After all, I had taken the buck fair and square from his backyard and on his terms. How could I possibly top that? ■

Kneel down, pick a spot, come to full draw, and take your shot.

MYTH: Even if you stand perfectly still, a buck will bolt as soon as he sees your human outline. After all, you don't belong in his part of the woods.

FACT: Who says you have to stand?

The real secret to shooting a buck from the ground at close range is to kneel down to take the shot. Of the twenty-odd whitetails I've arrowed while still-hunting, only three were taken while I was standing in an upright position.

As soon as you have a deer within range, you must drop to one knee, using any available vegetation or typography as cover, and nock an arrow. When you decide to shoot, first pick a spot and then slowly come to full draw when the buck is least likely to see the movement. Most of my shots have been 12 to 15 yards, but I have taken bucks much closer, including the seven-pointer I mentioned earlier.

Of course, a buck might see you kneeling there, but at close range, it is unlikely he will realize what you are before you release the shaft. A fully camouflaged "stump" at 15 yards simply does not look human!

Or, you could get that special look that shows the whites of his eyes, the look that says he knows he's been had but it's too late to do anything about it. You've then beat the master at his own game, and that is what makes still-hunting worth all the effort.

Telling the story over and over again!

3 Basic Equipment

The beauty of still-hunting is that unlike our treestand brethren we do not need a backpack full of gadgets to enjoy a day in the deer woods. Still-hunters travel light and go with the flow.

Keep it simple—that's the beauty of still-hunting. Indeed, if you intend to still-hunt with archery tackle, all you require besides a stout bow and a couple of razor-tipped arrows is a few accessories to help you get the job done properly. Our treestand brethren, however, don't have it so easy. They are often saddled with enough gadgets, doodads, and extraneous supplies to start their own archery pro shop! And they need these hunting accessories in order to be successful, or so they believe.

For example, in addition to lugging a portable treestand into the woods with them, treestand hunters will also tote a bag of tree steps, a pair of brush clippers, a package of glow-in-the-dark trail markers, a screw driver, an adjustable wrench, a pruning saw, a safety belt, a lift rope, a tree umbrella, a half-dozen scent dispensers, a bow hanger, a utility belt, an adjustable seat, a waterproof seat cushion, a full-size flashlight, a range finder, a pair of walkie-talkies, a canteen, and a pee bottle to their hunting site. And if that isn't enough to worry about, they will also bring a paperback novel to help them pass away the daylight hours. Imagine that—they get bored deer hunting!

If I decide to still-hunt the "back 40" for a couple of hours late in the afternoon, I will travel light, judging only three items to be essential. The first and most important is a quality pair of 8×30-class binoculars. As I mentioned earlier, not a mini pair, as they simply do not gather enough light at dawn or dusk, nor do they have a sufficient field of view to be anything more than an annoyance. And don't choose a full-size version that weighs several pounds, either. A quality pair of fit-in-the-hand, waterproof, shockproof, and dustproof glasses from Swarovski, Nikon, Leica, or Zeiss will let you scan the brush for a white throat patch or an antler tip all day long if need be without eye strain. They will run you between $500 and $1,000 dollars—money well spent when you consider the task at hand.

The second item I wouldn't leave camp without is a grunt tube. I hang at least one adjustable deer call around my neck plus I stuff a small single-purpose fawn bleat into my jacket pocket every time I enter the deer woods. Grunt tubes can be used as confidence calls whenever you stumble or crack a twig, but they can also be used to attract bucks to your present position. For a still-hunter, this means you can lure an unseen buck into shooting range or even turn a passing buck around in your direction. Either way, your day in the deer woods will be all that more remarkable when you remember to bring a grunt tube or two with you.

I was hooked on grunt tubes the first time I tried to call in a buck. It was late during the pre-rut, and the bucks were moving more and more during daylight hours. I heard what I believed to be a buck pass by near me and quickly blew two short notes on my grunt tube. The deer I heard was indeed a buck, and it charged in like a cop to a fistfight to investigate what he thought was another

Do you want to really blend into the forest? Then learn to talk to deer.

Mark your exact shooting location with flagging tape before you take up the blood trail to eliminate one of your biggest questions should blood and other sign be scarce—where precisely did I shoot from?

buck invading his turf. I was flabbergasted, to say the least, and never got an arrow nocked. Obviously, the buck escaped unscathed.

Since then, I have relaxed untold numbers of deer with my renditions of a fawn bleat and have called several bucks to within bow range with various buck-doe combinations. A grunt tube won't work every time you use it, but it has turned a buck's head often enough for me to consider it a necessary still-hunting accessory.

The third important item to bring still-hunting is fluorescent orange flagging tape. The first 20 minutes or so after a bowhunter takes a shot at a whitetail deer are often the most important in terms of recovery. Where exactly was the deer standing when the shot was made? How did the buck react to the shot? Where exactly did you last see the deer? Can you find the arrow?

Unlike a stand hunter, who after taking a shot can return to his treestand an hour later to reenact the episode, a still-hunter can easily forget exactly where he was positioned when he released the arrow. Was he standing next to that small oak, or was he kneeling a few yards away? Was the buck standing in front of or behind that big log?

To help you remember exactly where you and the deer were when you took your shot, it is important to immediately mark the spot from which you shot before you look for a blood trail. And nothing works better in this regard than a long strip of flagging tape left flapping in the breeze. The bright color can be seen from a great distance, and the plastic tape is impervious to rain or snow. And just as importantly, you can easily return to the flagging tape the next day if need be to continue the blood trail.

Fairly basic, huh? Sure, you might also want to stuff a topographical map and compass into a daypack if you were bowhunting the big woods, or a

Gore-Tex rain suit into a fanny pack if you were venturing into a new piece of property on a cloudy day. Nonetheless, you can still get by with fewer gadgets than if you were bowhunting from a treestand. And in my book, that leads to a simple, carefree day afield.

THE IDEAL STILL-HUNTING BOW

Some archery gear is undoubtedly better suited to sneak-and-peek deer hunting than other tackle—especially the bow. Indeed, the physical characteristics of some bows are conducive to still-hunting in the thick brush, whereas other models are ideal for still-hunting the wide-open spaces where cover is at a premium. There are still other bows that perform well from a treestand but are best left at home when it comes to still-hunting.

Which is a better choice then: a modern compound, a recurve, or a longbow? Well, that depends on how you expect your bow to perform in the wild. Here are the characteristics I think make a particular bow a good still-hunting weapon.

First, the tip-to-tip or axle-to-axle length should allow a still-hunter to shoot comfortably from unorthodox positions. My 62-pound Northwood

A good still-hunting bow is relatively short, allowing you to shoot accurately sitting or kneeling.

recurve, for example, is only 58 inches in length, yet I can shoot it just as accurately standing as I can kneeling down in the thick brush or squatting behind a tree stump. My compound is just over 40 inches in total length, and it, too, allows me to easily shoot in tight places.

As a rule of thumb, if you cannot shoot accurately from a sitting position in the deer woods, the bow is probably too long for you. And even if you are tall, a 60- to 65-inch longbow is simply too cumbersome in the thick brush to be a good still-hunting bow.

The second characteristic I look for in a still-hunting bow is the quiver. It should be attached to the bow in such a manner so it does not shake, rattle, or roll when you are carrying the bow, extracting an arrow shaft, or shooting. The hood should completely cover your broadheads, and it should be lined with felt or moleskin to help deaden any noise you might make preparing for the shot.

Stay away from back quivers and hip quivers, however. They may look cool, but they are quite troublesome in the deer woods. Back quivers tend to get hung up in the brush, and they do not hold arrows securely, whereas hip quivers give a still-hunter the pendulum effect. That is, the nocks and arrow's fletching swing back and forth as you walk like a pendulum on a clock.

Keep in mind that you do not need a full clip of arrow shafts to still-hunt effectively. Over the years there have only been three occasions where I released more than one arrow on any given day. Choose a light mini quiver that holds four to six shafts, and then carry only three or four razor-tipped hunting arrows with you afield. You won't regret it.

If you have your heart set on purchasing a new compound bow for still-hunting, I would recommend a finger bow. Still-hunting big game is a demanding sport, especially when it comes to eastern whitetails. When a shooting opportunity presents itself, you are often eyeball to eyeball with your prey. At this moment, you just don't have the time or the luxury to fiddle with a release. A still-hunter who chooses a tab can nock an arrow faster, quieter, and with less motion—and then get the shot off—than a bowhunter using a mechanical release.

The fourth characteristic I look for in a still-hunting bow is camouflage. Obviously, a flashy bow with bright colors will spook a buck into the next wood lot if you happen to wave it at him, but some all-wood bows can be just as much a giveaway. Fancy laminates and shiny finishes are meant to sell bows. You may have to spray paint your expensive recurve with dull paint if you ever expect it to draw blood.

Even modern compounds are not immune from the effects of shiny new advertising. What's the use of dipping a new bow with a designer-brand camouflage pattern if you are then going to imprint two-inch white lettering or the

Hip quivers are great for target practice around camp, but like back quivers, they can be quite troublesome in the deer woods.

company logo on the outside of both limbs? Waving this "camo" bow around in the deer woods is like flashing a white handkerchief. Use a felt marker or dull paint to cover the white lettering—or buy a different bow.

What about cam design? Draw weight? Let-off? For a smoother draw, choose a single cam over a hard cam, and then learn to shoot it with fingers. And do not overpower the bow. Adjust your draw weight so it is comfortable for you to shoot sitting down, kneeling down, and crouched over. After all, when the moment of truth finally presents itself, you want to be able to come to full draw from any unorthodox position smoothly and quickly without dropping an arrow off the rest.

Finally, if you are a compound aficionado, stay with the 65-percent let-off. Rarely will you have to hold the bow at full draw for extended periods of time. And on those rare occasions when you must—so what? That's bowhunting!

BOW SIGHTS

My friends and I first learned to shoot a bow and arrow by instinct. That is, we would stare at a leaf or a knot on a stump, come to full draw, and release a feathered shaft in one quick fluid motion. There were no compounds or aluminum shafts back then, nor were there any videos or television shows available to help us improve our shooting skills.

Then one day one of my pals taped a redheaded wooden matchstick to the riser of his recurve and started showing us how to put arrows into the kill zone on a regular basis. We soon learned to move our own match head up and down and then in and out until we were sighted in for 20 yards. It gave us accuracy we had only dreamed about, and it boosted our confidence when it came time to step afield.

Today, most still-hunters—indeed most bowhunters—use pins and a peep sight as a deadly a two-point aiming system. But a question soon arises. Is one pin enough, or is six too many? At first blush, this may seem to be a frivolous matter—until you start still-hunting whitetails. Then it becomes an issue. Let me explain.

One of the keys to successful still-hunting is learning to take advantage of subtle topographical features and available vegetation to get in close. Indeed, the average shot at an eastern whitetail is only 12 to 15 yards, with shots 25 yards and beyond quite rare. At these distances a good instinctive shooter is deadly, but so is a modern compound hunter wielding a single-pin bow. That's because today's wheel bows are incredibly fast and flat-shooting. When I am hunting deer with my compound, if I sight in the top of a single pin for 15 yards, then the middle of that pin is dead on at 23 yards, while the bottom can be effectively used for shots out to 28 yards. Thus, this single-pin setup covers nearly all contingencies.

If I am bowhunting whitetails in open farm country, however, or other big game animals such as moose or caribou in the wilds of Canada, then I might

Is one pin enough? Are six too many? You decide!

Instinctive shooting and still-hunting go together like peanut butter and jelly.

install a second pin and sight it in for 40 yards. I will then "split the pins" for shots between 28 and 40 yards and raise the 40-yard pin a pinch for slightly longer shots. Either way, a single or double pin is a deadly sight system for still-hunting with archery tackle.

The problem with a multiple-pin setup, however, is that it so often creates confusion at the moment of truth. Which pin is the right pin in any given situation? If the buck is uphill and 25 yards away, should you put your 20-yard pin right on his vitals, or should you aim low with a 30-yard pin? Indeed, is the buck really 25 yards away, or is it 31 yards? Keep in mind you are not sitting comfortably in a treestand waiting patiently for a buck to step into shooting range. Nor are you able to take advantage of manmade shooting lanes and laser rangefinders. You must act deliberately and quickly because you only have a moment or two to judge the distance, pick a spot, and come to full draw without being detected. Then you have to make the shot. The job is only made tougher if you have to deal with a fistful of multi-colored pins.

Then there is the time invested in sighting in and practicing with an array of pins. A bowhunter with six pins, for example, sighted in from 20 yards to 70 yards in 10-yard increments must spend an inordinate amount of time on the range zeroing in his sight system. This is time that could be better spent scout-

Air Bob soles offer tremendous traction over uneven terrain. Don't be tempted by impractical Madison Avenue designs.

ing his hunting grounds. Indeed, the best bowhunters I know—treestand hunters or still-hunters—spend most of their free time in the woods looking for deer and deer sign and their "spare" time target practicing.

But by far, the best reason to stay away from multiple-pin sight systems has more to do with the reason we still-hunt in the first place. Sure, there are easier ways to arrow a buck, and the biggest bucks don't generally fall to a still-hunter. But the pleasure I receive slipping up to within 20 yards of an unsuspecting whitetail buck, and then taking him fair and square, far outweighs any good vibrations I might receive from shooting a racked buck 50, 60, or more yards distant. The farther you are from the buck the less woodsmanship plays a role in your success.

Indeed, when you catch a buck flatfooted within easy bow range, you have already won the contest. You beat him by sharing the same wind currents, terrain features, and ground cover. And that is what makes you a good bowhunter and an expert still-hunter—not how far you can shoot!

BOOTS

Still-hunters spend a great deal of time sneaking about the deer woods over uneven terrain. They crawl up steep wooded hillsides, slip around swamps, and on occasion even leap over fallen logs. They also have to dig in to maintain their balance as they inch downhill on wet leaves or creep sideways under the rim of canyons and brush-strewn ravines. In fact, when still-hunting whitetail bucks, you often have to penetrate the most inhospitable habitat in order to get a clean shot. And to do that, you need solid footing.

This is where a boot sole fitted with Air Bobs or modified Air Bobs can help you stay the course. A heavy lug sole is a good second choice. Unfortunately, most modern boots have tread configurations that look like they were designed by kids who play video games after school rather than by experienced outdoorsmen. They simply do not give you the stability you need to still-hunt effectively over rough terrain. Indeed, most modern boot soles are not functional, and you can bet your last arrow these "cool" patterns have not been tested in the wild or the owners would have certainly broken their necks in the deer woods. Madison Avenue strikes again!

OUTERWEAR

Your outerwear must help keep you quiet in the deer woods. If you can "scratch" your jacket, pants, or gloves with a fingernail, then the clothing will simply not do. Branches, brush, and dry weed stems scraping against your body will give your position away every time.

Choose outerwear that is quiet in the deer woods. When in doubt, run a fingernail over the fabric. If it scratches, don't buy it.

To avoid being picked off by a buck's radar-like ears, brushed cotton in warm weather or wool when temperatures dip below freezing are your two best choices for remaining undetected. Fleece can be an acceptable alternative if you don't mind cleaning seeds, leaves, and grass stems from the fabric after a day afield—and you stay away from campfires.

Don't forget your hat! Knit caps tend to snag on brush, but a billed baseball cap of soft material can not only keep the sun out of your eyes, it can help deflect branches from your eyes as you tiptoe about. Your cap can also help break up your human outline. When I am in close proximity to a whitetail buck, I like to drop my head a bit and hide behind the bill. A human's close-set eyes spell "predator" to any deer. A hooded sweatshirt pulled loosely over your head can further camouflage your human form.

My final accessory for a full day afield still-hunting is a soft-faced fanny pack. In addition to my lunch and a bottle of water, I will stow an extra finger tab, a couple of grunt tubes, a rattle bag, orange flagging tape, a bottle or two of deer lure or urine, a spare arrow rest, a wad of toilet paper and a small flashlight—and if I am venturing into unfamiliar territory, a topographical map and compass, too. I might also toss in a box of waterproof matches, an onion, a sheet of aluminum foil, and packets of salt and pepper for the much anticipated heart and liver feast!

Finally, you may have thought I forgot to include a deer-dragging rig, but unless I am out to fill a doe tag, I plan on dragging my buck back to camp by the antlers. And if the antlers aren't big enough, I'll let him go to grow some that are!

How to Play the Wind ![4]

Native Americans were probably the best hunters to ever walk the North American continent. For thousands of years, they flourished in part because of their uncanny ability to put the sneak on unsuspecting big game animals, including white-tailed deer, and then kill them at close range. They knew then what many bowhunters are still grappling with today: to get the drop on a wary whitetail, you have to know how to play the wind.

Indeed, nothing spooks a deer faster than a snoot full of human stench. Unfortunately, many modern hunters don't know how to take the wind into consideration when attempting to move about the woods undetected. Sometimes, all it takes is predicting wind currents in advance, while at other times it takes changing direction in order to take into account a subtle shift or an errant breeze. Either way, playing the wind correctly is paramount to success and is the most challenging aspect of still-hunting.

The most challenging aspect of still-hunting is learning to play the wind correctly.

PREDICTABLE WINDS

The easiest winds to play correctly are those that are predictable in nature, and prevailing winds, steady winds, and thermals are the most important of these. If you can depend on the direction of the wind being constant, then it is easier for you to formulate a deadly ambush.

In my neck of the woods, the prevailing winds come out of the southwest. Under normal conditions, I can count on the wind to be consistently blowing from the same direction at a constant velocity each day I am afield. Thus, I can confidently park my 4×4 in the northeast quadrant of my hunting area to still-hunt my way upwind, or zigzag my way back and forth crosswind, to known concentrations of deer.

This also means that the bucks will be more or less moving along the same routes as usual. I can plan a still-hunting route ahead of time, for example, and then follow that route the next morning without having to change plans at the last minute to avoid spooking an otherwise relaxed deer.

This can be especially important if I want to sneak in and out of a buck's bedroom, a hot strategy late in the pre-rut. A sudden shift in wind direction at any time during the hunt could easily send a bedded buck hightailing it over the nearest ridge. But by depending on prevailing winds to remain on course without faltering, I manage each year to catch one or two bucks bedded down by working my way slowly crosswind through thickets, brush lots, and goldenrod fields known to harbor bucks during the middle of the day. This is always an exciting prospect, as most shot opportunities are less than 20 yards.

Smokestacks, flat water surfaces, and even grass stems can each help you determine current wind direction, an important factor in planning any day's hunt.

Keep in mind that bucks often bed in the same area under prevailing winds, making it easier for a still-hunter to get the drop on them.

A second type of predictable wind pattern is the steady wind. They usually blow from a different direction and at a greater velocity than prevailing winds and are generally the result of a storm front moving through the area. Steady winds of this nature may allow still-hunters the opportunity to hunt a different zone than usual.

A bedding area on one of the farms I hunt is difficult to get close to under a prevailing wind. I suppose that is one of the reasons the resident bucks chose this particular bailiwick. But when the winds swing and blow steady out of the northwest, I can still-hunt the edge of the bedding area with near impunity.

One fall, I took advantage of a change in prevailing wind direction and got the drop on a wide-racked 140-class ten-pointer I had glassed all summer long. The first time I saw him after the season opened he simply melted back into the brush without offering me a

A steady wind can help you still-hunt a particular ridge or river bottom with confidence.

shot. I was frustrated because you don't get too many chances at a buck like that. The good news, however, was that my airborne scent did not push him completely out of there, which kept open the opportunity of yet another close encounter.

The following week the winds again were out of the northwest, giving me a second chance at that record-book contender. I'd like to tell you I nailed him, but this time he caught me flat-footed, snorted, and then vamoosed in a flash. Big bucks not only pick bedding areas that are hard to reach, but they also seem to have a back-up plan in case you do manage to penetrate their stronghold. Indeed, we all know they don't get big by being careless!

Both prevailing winds and steady winds also offer careful still-hunters a great opportunity to sneak and peek through standing cornfields. Late morning and early afternoons are the best times to enter an uncut field. Why? For

Bedded bucks often have a backup plan should you penetrate their daytime hideout. An errant wind gave one of these bucks a second lease on life.

one, if there are bucks in the vicinity, they could very well have bedded somewhere in the field before first light. And two, a modest wind should rustle the leaves loud enough to help you camouflage your forward progress. A still-hunter moving through a cornfield under calmer conditions will only telegraph his whereabouts throughout the field, giving bedded deer more than enough time to escape.

Thermals are the third type of predictable wind pattern, and they are as easy to play to your advantage as prevailing winds and steady winds. Generally, as the sun rises in the morning, it warms the night air that has settled in the valley. Since that air is now lighter and less dense than the colder air, it rises uphill. Morning thermals continue racing uphill for the rest of the day until the sun begins to set in the afternoon. The air then soon cools, causing it to flow back downhill to the valley below. The easiest way to remember this pattern is to key in on the sun. That is, thermals rise uphill with the rising sun and then settle downhill with the setting sun.

How can a still-hunter best benefit from this phenomenon? Let's say your hunting grounds include a large alfalfa field bordered by hardwood ridges that harbor several bedded bucks during daylight hours. A rutting buck will probably dillydally around the alfalfa lot in the morning while trying to hook up with a hot doe. Then he will ride the thermals up the hill to his bedding grounds.

You can start at first shooting light by still-hunting back and forth just outside suspected bedding cover in the hopes of intercepting that buck before he reaches his security cover. If the thermals are strong that morning, however, he might just wind you and exit the area without you being aware of his presence.

Another option is to wait for the air in the valley to heat up, and then still-hunt downhill—and either crosswind or into the wind—but towards the feeding area along trails known to be used by family groups of does and fawns. If the buck has indeed hooked up with an estrous doe, you just might get a crack at him along one of those trails.

A still-hunter could also begin sneaking and peeking around the outside edge of the alfalfa lot at first shooting light, eventually working his way uphill at a crosswind angle in the hopes of intercepting that buck as it, too, slowly heads uphill and crosswind in its search for estrous does.

Later in the day, you can wait for the evening thermals to take hold before still-hunting crosswind outside his suspected bedding zone. You must wait for the change in wind to arrive, however, or your scent will be blown into the bedding area from daytime thermals, effectively alerting the buck to your presence.

Bucks use morning and evening thermals to their advantage when seeking estrous does. Follow his game plan to the T, and your chances of getting a shot soar.

MODERATE WINDS, STORMS, AND VARIABLE WINDS

Bowhunting predictable winds, be they prevailing, steady, or thermal, is more a science than an art, but logic is not always so apparent when dealing with winds that are unpredictable.

Look for bucks to be feeding in secluded orchards or on mast in steep ravines on cold, moderately windy days.

Take moderately windy days as an example. Coupled with frigid temperatures, deer will not normally feed out in the wide-open spaces, but will rather be found in pockets shielded by the bone-chilling winds. Indeed, if you don't see deer feeding out in the open on a cold, windy morning or evening, then look for them to be feeding out of the wind in abandoned apple orchards or in leeward ridges and steep ravines rich with acorns, beechnuts, and hickory mast.

If the winds pick up, expect deer to bed down in protected areas until the winds abate. They won't be relaxing, mind you. Their eyes, ears, and noses will be so overloaded with waving branches, crashing limbs, and odors that come and go that it will be hard for them to lie still without feeling threatened. Your best hope of getting a shot now is to be ready to hunt when the winds abate.

If the winds reach 30 or 40 miles per hour, all bets are off. Many deer will remain bedded down, but you are just as likely to see herds of deer out in the middle of open fields, where their sensory organs are not as challenged. Indeed, I've seen as many as twenty deer run out into a large open pasture one after another in mid-afternoon in an apparent attempt to escape the sensory overload in the woods.

Sometimes big bucks traveling solo can also be found on the move during days of high winds, especially during the rut. They seem oblivious to the sensory overload, or maybe that's how they react to all the stress. Whatever the case, you can often get away with making a lot of mistakes when hunting on days with high winds. These big bucks aren't able to see you, hear you, or smell you as well as they can when conditions are normal.

This doesn't mean that you are apt to get a clean shot. One year, I watched as a racked buck, jittery with all the limbs crashing about, passed by me within easy range. But when I loosened an arrow at him, he switched ends and walked away in the opposite direction before the arrow ever reached him. When threatened, bucks in high winds can still react amazingly fast.

Another problem you will encounter on days of high winds is arrow drift. The air will push the arrow off target in much the same way wind will cause a bullet to drift. I once missed an easy 20-yard shot at a relaxed animal when I foolishly took a shot on a very windy day. I can still see the shaft sailing behind and over the animal's back by several feet!

Of course, major storms are another matter. To still-hunt outside a feeding area or along a hot scrape line when the wind is blowing hard enough to bring Dorothy from *The Wizard of Oz* crashing down is usually an exercise in

The good news is that rutting bucks are often on the prowl despite high winds. More good news: their primary senses are often overloaded, making them more vulnerable to still-hunting.

futility. The deer just aren't normally moving around much on such days. You could sneak through bedding areas, but the deer are so spooky even a crashing branch will send them off on a run. Your best bet is to wait until the storm wanes. Bucks will be up and about then, especially during the rut, giving you a better than even opportunity.

Without a doubt, the most difficult time to drop a buck is when the winds are variable. If you are still-hunting, the constant change in direction and velocity will make it all but impossible to keep the wind in your favor. All you will manage to do on days like this is jump deer from one protected pocket to another. You are much better off staying in camp, catching up on odd chores and lost sleep. To better understand this phenomenon, try drifting a feather, leaf, or milkweed seeds on days of variable winds to see how these fickle currents can raise havoc with scent control.

In summary, early Americans used sweat baths to purge their bodies of unwanted odors. They then smeared plant and animal juices on themselves before draping animal skins, sometimes green, over their shoulders to help keep their human odor at bay. But to be consistently successful, they still had to play the wind.

Bowhunters must avoid shots much over 15 yards on windy days. A perfect shot may turn into a marginal hit due to arrow drift.

Set some milkweed free on a windy day to see how easy gentle wind currents can spread your scent about.

Of course, those early hunters did not have to contend with sweet-smelling soaps and shampoos in their clothing, gas and oil drippings on their moccasins, and short hunting seasons. That's why modern man often uses scent-free soaps and shampoos, scent-eliminator sprays, and scent-absorbing clothing to help keep his human odor to a minimum. But like the early Americans, to be consistently successful, you still have to pay attention to the wind and learn to play it correctly.

5 Sounds of Silence

We learn early to keep our eyes open if we want to see more deer. Well, you can see even more bucks if you learn to keep your ears open, too!

CRACK! CRACK! That sound stopped me dead in my tracks. It was not a gray squirrel, of that I was sure, nor was it a bird hunter walking along on the far side of the creek. The cadence was simply out of step with man hunting ruffed grouse. It was something big, however, and it was emanating from a nearby thicket.

I glassed the brush, looking for a big critter of some sort, when the sounds of leaves and twigs being tossed into the air suddenly permeated the woods. Was it a buck, I wondered, making a scrape? I listened intently now and was about to go take a look-see when I heard a couple of deep guttural grunts. I knew then what it was and looked over the creek just in time to see the buck exit the patch of brush and disappear over the ridge. I later inspected the thicket and found a fresh scrape still steaming from the morning's action.

This heart-thumping action took place early in my still-hunting career, teaching me an important lesson: undisturbed bucks often make lots of noise as they go about their daily business. Some of these sounds are easy to decipher, such as a buck walking through dry leaves, while others tend to be more obscure and difficult to comprehend, such as a buck pawing through snow looking for fallen mast. Whatever the case, the more deer sounds you can identify in the wild the more likely you are to anticipate a buck's presence before he actually steps into view.

FEEDING SOUNDS

Bucks make all kinds of noise when they are feeding. The most distinctive sound is the cadence of their steps. A feeding deer does not walk along in a predictable fashion, that is, he does not take steps that are unidirectional and equidistant in nature. Quite the contrary, each step is separated by long pauses, giving him ample time to browse on twigs or to scoop up acorns lying on the ground. After gathering what food is readily available, he will then move left, right, or straight ahead to the next morsel, taking only as many steps as necessary and often pushing leaves aside with his snout as he searches for more food at ground level. The next time you are afield pay close attention to deer as they feed by you, and put that cadence to memory. It will serve you well on future hunts.

Bucks make a distinctive sound chomping down on apples and hard mast. Once you hear it, you won't forget it.

The type of food a buck happens to be eating can also be a dead giveaway to his position. An examination of a buck's stomach contents, for example, will show you that apples are usually swallowed in small chunks. Acorns are also chewed up pretty well and are rarely swallowed whole or even halved. That means there's a whole lot of chewing going on, and if you listen carefully, you might be able to hear a buck actually chomp down on his food. Soft mast such as apples and pears pop and splatter as a buck feeds, whereas when a buck chows down on hard mast like acorns, beechnuts, or hickory nuts, you'll hear a more distinctive "woody" sound accompanying each bite.

While more than one buck has announced his arrival because of noisy eating habits in the woods, nothing makes more noise than a buck eating corn right off the stalk. They often first pull or yank down individual ears, shaking the whole plant in the process, before tearing off the tender tips. You might not be able to see the buck, but you can pretty well pinpoint his whereabouts and direction of travel by keeping your ears open. Indeed, a buck feeding in a cornfield makes almost as much noise as a family of raccoons!

One late summer evening while scouting for deer I heard a different sound, a "snip-snip-snip," that had me baffled before I saw a buck less than 20 yards away biting the tops off of green goldenrod plants. Another time, I listened as a buck picked a dead leaf off a bush and consumed it rather greed-

A buck working his way along a hardwood ridge in dry leaves has a particular cadence that we all can identify. Now take that one step further and begin listening for the sounds bucks make as they wade through cattails, goldenrod, or standing corn.

ily. The plucking noise followed by the crinkling of a single leaf was quite distinctive. Now, if I pick up an unfamiliar sound in the deer woods, I stop and look around carefully. You never know when you will stumble upon a buck feeding nonchalantly nearby.

HOOF BEATS

There are other sounds besides the feeding cadence that you can use to help identify the whereabouts of a racked deer. An obvious example is a buck crossing a stream. You can often hear each individual hoof being dabbed into the water, along with splashing, and then the hooves clawing their way up the stream bank.

With practice you can pinpoint the exact location of deer by simply listening for the unusual sounds they make as they go about their daily routines.

Bucks also make distinctive sounds when they travel through vegetation. In the early season, the sound of a buck traveling through goldenrod is quite different than the sound of a buck working his way through goldenrod that has dried and turned brittle. Indeed, various types of vegetation have their own "signature" sound when a buck passes through, and it is to your advantage to catalog these in your brain. When in doubt what these sounds might be, just listen to the noises *you* make as you hoof it through a grown-over field, a brushy hedgerow, or a mud-spattered beaver dam.

Over the years I have identified the presence of many bucks by simply keeping my ears open to all kinds of unusual sounds. Examples include the "twang" of a buck jumping over a barbed-wire fence or the sounds of a buck's rack scraping against a strand of wire as he crawls under a barbed fence. Stone walls are a dead giveaway, too, if you can strain your ears to hear a buck's hooves clatter on the stones, and then the "thud" of him landing on the other side.

One of the more intriguing noises we all seem to hear during the deer season are the sounds of a spooked buck bounding away towards heavy cover.

To keep your presence a secret from a buck's swiveling ears, ditch the ATV and get a golf cart. They are the stealth aircraft of the deer woods.

I say buck here because if you listen carefully you can often tell if the deer you jumped was a buck or a doe. A mature buck is a heavy animal, and with practice, you should be able to differentiate between the dainty sounds of a 100-pound doe bolting along a ridge and the thundering hoof beats of a 200-pound mature buck hightailing it into the swamp. If you cup your ears, you might also determine how far the buck ran and whether he looped to the left or right before stopping. And if the brush is thick, you might also hear the sounds of his rack slapping branches as he makes good his escape.

Of course, man is not the only thing that causes bucks to run. During the rut you might hear one or more bucks chasing a single doe around and around. At first, you might think you spooked those deer, but if you listen carefully, you might hear the doe bleat a few times or the tending grunts of one of the bucks as he tries to close the distance between him and the doe.

A couple of years ago I was sneaking along the edge of a river when I heard something bounding up and down the river bank, and then cross the river back and forth in huge gushing bounds. What troubled me about this noise was that if it were a deer, it was crossing where the water was deepest and not in the shallows where I would have expected a crossing to occur. Well, it was a buck all right, chasing a doe, but not any ordinary buck. It was the biggest eight-pointer I have ever seen in the wild, a Boone & Crockett contender to be sure. I'd like to tell you I arrowed that buck, but he ended up on the other side of the river, and there was no place for me to safely cross to go after him.

SOUNDS OF LOVE

In addition to chasing does around, bucks make other characteristic noises during the rut that can help you pinpoint their exact whereabouts. So unique are these sounds that if you like to still-hunt as I do, then it would always behoove you to immediately sneak over and investigate as soon as you hear any of them.

The first sound to listen for in the autumn deer woods is a buck making a rub. It is a faint scraping noise, but once you hear the bark being shredded off a sapling, you will have no trouble identifying what is going on, especially if the scraping noises are accompanied by occasional buck grunts. If you are not sure of your ears, and wonder if they are not playing tricks on you, then look for the swaying of a nearby sapling or small tree. That should be all the convincing you need. In fact, one season I took a closer look-see at just such a swaying sapling and ended up arrowing a fat eight-pointer in his bed.

The second sound to listen for during the breeding season is a buck making a scrape. Like rub making, a buck pawing away at the earth also grunts a bit. Those grunts, along with the sounds of forest duff being tossed away from the scrape, can help disguise your forward progress, but you must still be careful. One year while photographing wild bucks in Ontario, Canada, I heard the telltale sounds of scrape making, and using a grunt tube, I zeroed in for a picture. The buck, not sure what I was, cocked his head, lowered it to the ground, and charged, scaring the pudding out of me. I escaped unharmed, but it taught me a lesson: if you are going to sneak up on a rutting buck, shoot him or leave him alone. A rut-crazed buck is nothing to fool with!

Finally, you must also keep your ears peeled for two bucks sparring. It is surprising how close you can get to the scene of the action if you take your time and cover your forward progress with an occasional fawn or doe bleat. Both combatants are usually so preoccupied that you can get right on top of them!

I have been able to work myself to within bow range of sparring bucks on several occasions, but I have not always been fortunate

Rutting bucks can be located by the sounds they make rubbing trees, clearing scrapes, and jousting. Learn to identify and then mimic this clatter.

If you hear what you believe to be two bucks fighting, listen carefully. If the sequence lacks realism, then back off. It might just be your neighbor. If it sounds authentic, then proceed with caution. It might just be my neighbor!

enough to get a shot, in part because these shoving matches rarely take place in the open but rather in overgrown fields or brush lots. Even so, correctly identifying the action and then getting close enough to confirm your suspicions is a thrill few deer hunters ever experience. Over the years I have passed on several bucks sparring because I couldn't get a clean shot. I did manage to tag two others that were too busy keeping an eye on each other to notice me kneeling at full draw in the shadows!

Another word of caution is in order. Rattling has become a popular technique not only for bowhunters early in the season but for gun hunters, too. Generally, I can tell if a human is clashing antlers because they go about their rattling too fast, too loud, too often, and without any ancillary sounds to help authenticate their efforts, such as fake hoof beating or buck grunting. Even so, listen carefully, and if you have any doubt about the realism of the sparring match, then back away. You don't want to ruin a fellow hunter's setup, and you don't want to become his target either, especially if you come sneaking in with the aid of a grunt tube!

So learn to keep your ears open to the unusual, the curious, and the unbelievable, and then catalog those sounds in your brain for future reference. Over time, you will undoubtedly see more bucks.

How to Beat Buck Fever

6

The smile on his face says it all. He beat buck fever and bagged the buck of a lifetime.

S ome call it a simple case of the shakes—nothing to really worry about—while others define these uncontrollable wiggles and jerks as nothing less than a full-blown illness in need of expert medical intervention. No matter how you interpret the symptoms, one thing is for certain—buck fever is real.

Doubt me? Just visit an autumn deer camp, and you will hear the tales of woe about the monster buck that was caught dead in his tracks only to escape unscathed. Or about the poor hunter who got so nervous his knees buckled when a tall-tined buck suddenly appeared out of nowhere. Indeed, it makes little difference if you are a seasoned veteran or a newcomer to the sport; sooner or later, every deer hunter gets a good dose of buck fever.

An encounter with buck fever can take many forms. Some bowhunters, for example, get so flustered they almost fall out of their treestands when the moment of truth presents itself. Others, despite their best efforts, cannot seem to come to full draw at their first sight of a trophy buck, while still others start shaking so badly they can't even nock an arrow when they hear leaves crunching behind

A "shooter" about to get away is often all it takes to trigger an episode of buck fever.

their stand. Even a mild confrontation can result in difficulty breathing, sweaty palms, dry mouth, and an inability to speak coherently.

What is buck fever? Buck fever is really nothing more than an acute anxiety attack, a conflict of thought and feelings exacerbated by the sight of a white-tailed deer, although the sight of any hunted critter can elicit similar symptoms.

That's right, it's the "touchy-feely" stuff that we macho males often have a hard time understanding. In a nutshell, a psychic conflict arises between what we think and how we feel about a given set of circumstances. (Interestingly enough, if you are a target shooter, it's called target panic.)

For example, we may brag to the guys at deer camp what great shots we are, but secretly we feel differently. We may have real doubts, for instance, about our shooting abilities, as evidenced by a feverish preoccupation with owning the right equipment or the need to tell everyone in camp over and over again about our prowess on the target range. In these cases, we *think* we are a good shot and we want desperately to be a good shot, but deep down inside, in our heart of hearts, we *feel* quite insecure.

In other cases, we may fear success and all its ramifications, or we may even have an unconscious desire to punish ourselves for past "sins." In still other cases, a miss can be a positive event because it brings notice to an attention-seeking individual. As a former psychotherapist for the U.S. government, I saw many variations on these themes from patients suffering from anxiety-related disorders.

As alluded to earlier, there is also a physiological component to buck fever—the racing heart and sweaty palms. Up until just recently, social scientists had no data on the physiological aspects of an actual deer hunt. Then in 1997, University of Wisconsin-Madison graduate student Richard C. Stedman and rural sociologist Thomas A. Heberlein devised a groundbreaking experiment to gather just that.

Stedman and Heberlein hypothesized "that encounters with game will produce measurable physiological response in hunters. More specifically, hunters should respond more strongly when game is present than when it is absent; the strongest response should occur when directly engaged in shooting at prey."

They divided the hunting experience into four parts based on a hunter's interaction with game, and then fitted ten volunteers aged 26 to 62 with heart monitors. Stedman and Heberlein then took them waterfowl hunting, upland bird hunting, and deer hunting.

The results were not surprising, at least to those of us who love to hunt: encounters with game strongly affected heart rates. When game was not present, the mean heart rate was 90.9 beats per minute (bpm) across all types of game. When game was present but no shots were taken, mean heart rate increased to 97.5 bpm. When shots were taken but missed, the average heart rate rose to 113.5 bpm, and when game was killed, the heart rate was

Buck fever reaches its most feverish pitch just as we are about to shoot at a buck.

Sharing the hits and misses with family and friends at deer camp can at times help alleviate the symptoms of buck fever.

112.4 bpm. The difference between not seeing game and successful/unsuccessful shooting at game was significant, as was the difference between seeing game and shooting at game.

Also not surprising was the fact that deer produced the biggest jumps in heart rates, from 78 bpm with no game in sight, to 100 bpm when sighted, to 122 bpm at the shot. Indeed, merely seeing deer produced significant effects even if no shot was taken.

Stedman's and Heberlein's research also suggests there is a one-two punch that reinforces the act of deer hunting. That is, there is a social component to hunting that can act in a positive fashion—the proverbial slap on the back when a hunter returns from the field with a buck.

Thus the physiological responses, of which increased heart rates was the only one studied, combined with the many social aspects of deer hunting, such as traditional camp life, are probably what attracts and holds so many of us to deer hunting.

FIGHT OR FLIGHT

Why is an increase in heart rate (bpm) important? There is a linkage between increased heart rates and the production of epinephrine, more commonly known as adrenaline, which is responsible for the "flight or fight" response in animals. Too much epinephrine and the inability to keep it under control are believed to contribute to anxiety or panic disorders in humans.

Keep in mind that a sudden increase in epinephrine does not necessarily lead to an anxiety or panic attack. It is a "flight *or* fight" phenomenon. If under control, the sudden influx of epinephrine can lead to super-human strength of heroic proportions, such as lifting a full-size automobile off a trapped human—or making that shot of a lifetime on a rapidly escaping record-book buck.

When it comes time to make the shot, we either buckle down and do the deed or fold under the pressure and shake uncontrollably.

A deer hunter, for instance, can become very excited when it comes time to shoot at a buck, but not so excited that he is panic-stricken and blows the shot. As Stedman and Heberlein point out, the increase in heart rate probably prepares a predator for the chase; it does not necessarily doom the predator to failure.

COPING MECHANISMS

We know that an unresolved psychic conflict—no matter what the dynamics—coupled with acute physiological symptoms, such as a racing heart and spastic muscle movements, can cause us to blow an easy 20-yard broadside shot. So what can you do? Well, apart from intensive individual or group psychotherapy, you can begin by being brutally honest with yourself. Are you afraid others will laugh at you or ridicule your hunting achievements? Are you really the woodsman you say you are? No, really? Not sure? Then ask your spouse or a trusted hunting buddy for an opinion. Their trusted remarks might offer you some insight into your experience with buck fever.

I said earlier that buck fever can attack any hunter, experienced or neophyte. But the more experience you have as a deer hunter the less likely you are to experience an attack. A sight of a fork-horn, for example, might excite a youngster on his first hunt, but it is unlikely to get an old timer's heart to beat wildly.

A hunter with a few years in the field and a few bucks under his belt might get nervous and jerky when a wide-racked record-book ten-pointer saunters past his stand just out of range. But a deer hunter with twice the experience might just take it in stride, knowing full well that big bucks don't get big by being stupid. This will allow him to sit back and drink in the experience, knowing that given the right set of experiences he may very well get another opportunity at such an animal.

What gets the experienced hunter in trouble is when he is confronted with Old Mossy Horns himself, the buck of a lifetime. Visions of grandeur often dance in his head. Money, fame, and the right to claim he is the best deer hunter in the state are his if only he can pull off the shot. But then, you guessed it, because of some unresolved psychic conflict, he plucks the string, sending an arrow harmlessly off into the wild blue yonder.

Experience in the deer woods generally lessens the chance of a full-blown attack of buck fever.

The number one reason hunters miss is buck fever.

Dr. Warren Strickland, pro staffer for PSE Archery, has arrowed trophy-quality big game animals all across North America plus several species in Africa. His prescription, if you will pardon the phrase, is really what the doctor ordered: "The most common reason trophy animals are missed is not because the critter smells you, hears you, or even sees you out of the corner of his eye," says Strickland. "It is because you flinch, fail to pick a spot, or exhibit uncharacteristic poor shooting form due to an attack of buck fever. You cannot wait until the deer shows up to think about controlling this ancient malady. It can simply be too late by then. Instead, you must learn to deal with buck fever before the buck steps into view. Sure, it can help to rehearse the hunt mentally

Friendly shooting contests and 3-D tournaments can help you deal more effectively with anxiety associated with deer hunting.

by imaging the buck approaching your stand, and then going through all the steps of picking a spot, drawing your bow, and releasing a broadhead. But there is no substitute for putting yourself in pressure-cooker-like situations to help you learn to deal effectively with your anxieties.

"Keep in mind that we all get that adrenaline rush," adds Strickland. "That's why we enjoy bowhunting whitetail deer and other big game animals, but we must learn to keep it under control. It can be very frustrating when we let buck fever dig its claws into us. Indeed, repeated bouts of buck fever can easily destroy anybody's confidence levels.

"Keep in mind, too, that we usually only get one chance at a big-game animal, so we have to learn to make the most of it. And in this vein, learning to control buck fever is as important as target practicing, scouting, and putting a stand up in a killer location. For example, 3-D tournaments are an excellent way to learn to deal with pressure and anxiety. Only in this case it is peer pressure, the kind that can leave you tense and sweaty whenever you have to shoot in front of other people. Better to get the kinks out now than to have to deal with it during the bowhunting season.

"Better yet, get used to being close to deer before the season by spending more time in the woods scouting and photographing deer. Wildlife photography can be an excellent way to help you feel comfortable in close proximity to deer. Indeed, getting the drop on a monster buck during the off-season can desensitize you to a close encounter later in the fall. Be aware, however, that one of the biggest mistakes a bowhunter can make is becoming a trophy hunter too early in his career. To get to the point where you feel comfortable in close proximity to a trophy buck, you have to first feel at ease when you are within bow range of does and fawns. Don't put the cart before the horse!

"What can you do if you are nonetheless struck by buck fever?" asks Strickland. "When the adrenaline is running through your body like wildfire, think about something other than bowhunting. Take yourself out of the heat of the battle by concentrating on something less threatening. Everyone has their own way, but I try not to look at the animal, and in the case of big whitetail bucks, I avoid staring at that rack! You must struggle to keep your emotions under your hat!

One way to control the shakes is to concentrate on something soothing, like a day at the beach. Don't look at those horns or all will be lost!

How many of these hunters will experience buck fever in their lifetime? Virtually all of them!

"Unfortunately," adds Strickland, "hunters today put too much pressure on themselves. They save their money for five years to book a hunt, and then expect to take an animal home with them. You must understand that what you are paying for is the experience; you are not buying an animal. Fortunately, with maturity comes the realization that you do not have to fill a tag to have a great hunt. Indeed, a lot of the fun surrounding big game bowhunting occurs way before a critter ever steps into view! This knowledge alone can help you stay focused during a close encounter with a big game animal.

"I have learned over the years that the very best bowhunters, those that seem to be successful from one season to the next, are not the nervous types, but rather quite the opposite. They are laid-back and calm. Nothing really bothers them. They do their homework, they target practice, and they have their emotions under control when an opportunity presents itself."

Now there's a prescription that is easy to swallow!

PART II
Still-Hunting
Strategies

Cutting Corners: Still-Hunting New Property

7

There was magic in the air. To my right was a series of hogbacks covered in thick, purple haze while to my left stood a plateau overlooking a sparkling creek and a dense stand of conifers. And in front, a long and winding valley seemed to disappear from view only to reappear further up the hollow in the form of a lush, hillside meadow. Could this be the place, I wondered?

I raised my Swarovski 8×30s and took a closer look. The hogbacks were covered with hardwoods—some of them definitely oaks—with no evidence of recent logging. The plateau was crisscrossed with hedgerows and abandoned farm fields. A tractor trail led down to the creek. And in the valley, a barbed-wire fence in obvious need of repair was strung out along the wooded north border, ending at a gray, two-story farmhouse and a cluster of ramshackle outbuildings. A collection of old cars and rusted farm machinery, sentinels to an era long past, rested near one of the

Whitetails thrive on a good mix of hardwoods, abandoned fields, and active farmland.

barns. Yes, there was magic in the air, a kind of magic that spells one word to me: whitetail!

When I first found this paradise a few years back, I couldn't believe my good fortune. Much of the land was a state wildlife management area, and I later acquired written permission to deer hunt those adjacent acres under private control. As it turned out, there were bucks everywhere, but best of all, there were no other bowhunters patrolling the property. I had this deer-rich heaven all to myself!

I couldn't wait to still-hunt here with my bow and arrow, but first I needed to do some research. You see, still-hunting requires a set of strategies that differs a great deal from sitting high in a tree. For example, a treestand hunter might want to set up inside a finger of brush that protrudes into one of the meadows, or at a creek crossing near those conifers. But a still-hunter must cover much more ground, taking careful advantage of the topography and all available ground cover to get in close for a shot.

Study the juxtaposition of various features such as ravines and plateaus on your topographical map. Do you see any natural travel corridors?

ORIENTATION

How do you still-hunt property you've never set foot on before? Well, you could get lucky by simply stumbling around—if you have all the time in the world. Even if you didn't get a deer, you would certainly know the woods like the back of your hand by season's end.

Or, you could cut some corners by first learning to read aerial and topographical maps. This is where you get your first clues as to the general whereabouts of mature bucks, including preferred feeding areas, travel routes, bedding locations, and those hard-to-find hotspots most likely to display signs of the rut later in the fall.

To get started, cruise the periphery of your prospective new hunting grounds, either by foot or vehicle. Stop wherever you get a view and orient your position with topographical map and compass. To do this correctly, simply set an orienteering compass at 360 degrees and place it on the map so that the side edge of the

Don't overlook public land for trophy deer. A buck might have an offbeat hideout that allows him to feed after dark but remain undetected during daylight hours.

base plate lies parallel with the magnetic north line of the declination diagram found in the margin of your map. The direction of the travel arrow should point toward north. Then turn the map with the compass lying on it until the north part of the compass needle points to the N of the compass housing. The compass and map (and you) are now oriented.

Next, pick out visible landmarks in front of you, such as a hilltop, a creek, or a steep ridge, and find them on the map. Then study the relationships between these various landmarks. What is the distance between these points of interest? What is the shortest route between points? What is the most likely route between points? Using your aerial maps, what role does ground cover play in each of these locations? These are important steps in getting to know the lay of the land, and more importantly, where the bigger bucks live.

BIOLOGIST

Next, show your maps to the local deer biologist—the most under-utilized asset in the deer hunter's arsenal. Although it is unlikely he or she will show you exactly where to hunt, a biologist will be able to add some details to your maps that you might have otherwise been unaware of, making them more meaningful. For example, ask about boundaries for public land holdings and about any new holdings that may have been added to the public domain. Any property that was once off limits to hunting could be a sanctuary for giant deer. Ask, too, about access to these lands during inclement weather. Will you need a 4×4 equipped with power winch and chains, or will the family sedan suffice?

Ask about the existence of new beaver dams, clear-cuts, blow-downs, landslides, forest fires, and logging operations, all of which create new forest growth that attract deer. Ask him or her to draw these features on your map for you.

Finally, ask how the deer have fared during the past three or four winters. Couple this to questions concerning fawn survival, buck-to-doe ratios, hunting pressure, poaching, and reports of trophy deer. What about this year's mast crop? As you can see, one question should lead to another, leaving you vastly better acquainted with your new hunting grounds.

FEEDING SITES

I like to begin by keying in on overgrown fields and abandoned orchards in farm country, and hardwood ridges and creek bottoms in the big woods. You'll find the freshest sign in these feeding sites early in the season, and again after the rut.

Ask the landowner, local biologist, or even the rural letter carrier for hints where deer might be congregating. Then check it out.

Overgrown fields are often located adjacent to old farm buildings. Look on your topographical map for small openings with 90-degree corners and the symbol for a building, a black box, nearby. Deer like to enter these fields near corners and along any dip in terrain that offers them cover.

You can still-hunt the nearby edges and take advantage of the same cover, but stay in the shadows and never cross through the middle of an opening. Instead, walk in the tall grass, along fence lines, or inside deep furrows left by the plow so you can hide the back-and-forth action of your feet and legs. Remember, a buck's eyes are geared to pinpoint movement.

Still-hunt cautiously through overgrown fields and old orchards by sticking to the shadows.

Another hot feeding site is an orchard, and the longer it has been neglected the better. The topographical map symbol for an orchard is multiple rows of irregular green circles. They are drawn to look like treetops when viewed from above. You'll find deer almost anywhere in an orchard, so I concentrate on working it methodically, one row at a time. Walk very slowly and stay low. Stone walls, dirt mounds, brush piles, large rocks, and natural depressions often provide additional cover.

And stay alert. Thick, overgrown apple orchards are great places to catch a buck milling about 30 minutes or so before sunset. Bucks like to use these ancient orchards as staging areas if they are adjacent to a large opening frequented by does and fawns. I once caught a fat eight-pointer flatfooted in an old orchard as he waited for the sun to set, but the thick vegetation made it impossible for me to draw and shoot. He finally passed within 10 yards of me on his way to a nearby meadow, never knowing how close he had come to death.

If there is a mast crop in the big woods, ridges and high-ridge plateaus are the places to still-hunt an unsuspecting buck. In the evening, bucks will sometimes use an acorn-laden ridge or plateau as a staging area before descending into the valley below, and in the morning, he may just dillydally long enough right after first light for you to get a shot at him before he beds down.

The trick to still-hunting ridges is to sneak along with only your head showing above the crest. This minimizes the chances of a buck catching sight of your forward progress. Pay close attention to the leading edges of plateaus, too. These are often natural bottlenecks, excellent places to take your time. And keep your ears open. More than one buck has met his demise because an alert hunter listened for that telltale *crunch-crunch-crunch* of a buck feeding on fallen mast.

BEDDING AREAS

Mature bucks like to bed in those thick tangles most hunters avoid. That's one reason they've gotten so big. If you find yourself going around a large patch of cover—like a swamp or brush-choked ravine—you may have stumbled onto a good bedding area.

In farm country, start by locating un-tillable terrain on your topographical map. Creek beds, steep hillsides, and ravines are impossible to plow, and combined with the thick vegetation that inevitably thrives here, they offer deer ample protection from human intrusion. A close proximity to active agriculture is always a plus.

Stay below the crest of the ridge and you lessen your chances of being picked off by a wary buck.

Bucks generally bed high and feed low, but if there is thick cover at the base of the mountain and a bumper crop of mast on the hardwood ridges above, then some bucks might very well bed low and feed high.

Deer generally bed high and feed low in the big woods, so scan your map for hilltops—and those benches that sometimes lie just below—for probable bedding sites. Ravines, canyons, and small islands inside a swamp are good places to expect a buck to bed, too. Don't overlook clear-cuts. Some big old bucks find that clear-cuts often offer them enough food, water, and cover to make it their core area, exposing themselves only after darkness.

Once the rut is underway, bedding areas frequented by family groups of does and fawns become magnets for amorous bucks. Try sneaking in and out of the edges in the early morning right after a storm front. You generally want to stay out of bedding areas at other times of the season, but I've had good luck working bedding sites when it is raining, snowing, or just plain windy. The trick is to still-hunt crosswind. Bucks generally bed facing downwind with their backs to heavy cover. If you only hunt into the wind, they will easily spot your forward progress and vamoose well before you step into bow range.

TRAVEL ROUTES

"Eureka!" That's what most hunters say when they realize they can predict a buck's preferred travel route by simply studying a topographical or aerial map. Aerial photos can help pinpoint crossings where vegetation is a factor,

Still-hunting along a travel route is a sure-fire tactic for farmland and big-woods whitetails. Look for terrain features and waist-high vegetation to steer you in the right direction.

especially in farm country where fingers of brush, hedgerows, and adjoining blocks of woods often dictate direction of travel.

In the big woods, however, it is more often the lay of the land that bucks prefer to follow, and the astute map reader can quickly choose a path for a morning's still-hunt by simply studying the various relationships between those brown squiggly lines. What you are looking for are terrain features that put the squeeze on a buck, like a natural funnel, or features that allow him to save calories, like the easiest path up a mountain.

Try the saddles between high peaks, gentle slopes leading into steep canyons, the uppermost tips of ravines, spurs that lead to creek crossings, steep ridges adjacent to lakes and streams, and hardwood ridges that drop down into swamps. If you can string a couple of these together, you have the makings of a morning or evening still-hunt.

Once you spot a couple of natural travel routes on your maps, others will quickly materialize. In fact, with a little practice, they are as easy to find as your name in the telephone book. Still-hunting some travel routes is tough because cover is sometimes sparse, and the deer are not as concentrated as they are around bedding areas and feeding sites. When I still-hunt a travel route, I stick to the shadows and stop next to anything that can help break up my outline, such a large tree or a blow-down.

As you might expect, the moment of truth is risky, too. The trick here is to take your shot kneeling down, and the closer to a tree trunk or clump of brush the better. You're just another stump then; not a six-foot human waving his funny looking legs about.

SIGNS OF THE RUT

Finding scrapes, scrape lines, rubs, and rub lines can be tough, especially in the big woods when there is so much cover to examine. You can narrow your search if you know the vegetation and terrain features bucks seem to seek

A fresh rub can give you clues as to where a buck is feeding and maybe bedding down. This one was found along the edge of a field, however, telling you only that a decent buck is working the area.

when the rut begins. Think of where you have found "buck works" in the past, and then try to find similar locations on either of your maps.

Any block of woods in farm country is a candidate for buck sign, but I pay particularly close attention to unusual features within that wood lot, such as a small ridge or a long narrow depression, to help me locate fresh buck sign. Of course, streambeds, the bottom of brushy ravines, and secluded orchards are always worth a look-see, too.

The corners of large clear-cuts, especially if they are dotted with spruce and hemlock, are good places to find breeding sign in the big woods, as are the saddles between high peaks, damp ground adjacent to steep ridges, and dilapidated jeep trails. These are all easy to locate on a topographical map.

My favorite tool for finding buck sign in the big woods is the aerial map. Small openings in the understory seem to attract rutting bucks more than any other feature. These are often the result of age-old clear-cuts and long-forgotten logging roads, but several uprooted trees can also leave an opening large enough to attract 250-pound whitetails.

Scrape lines are death traps for a rutting buck, if you can decipher when he is likely to return. Don't dillydally—still-hunt along the line the very next time you expect the buck to reappear.

The trick to still-hunting rut sign is to do so the very next time you expect the buck to appear. If you wait until tomorrow or next weekend, the buck may very well be in the company of an estrous doe. Scrape lines are generally good for a week to ten days. In farm country, the buck will probably be around for most of that time, but in the case of the big woods, he may be 10 miles away tending another scrape line on another ridge above another clear-cut for several days before he decides to return.

In summary, your best chance of tagging a buck by still-hunting with a bow and arrow is the very first time you set foot on a piece of property. Why not use your topographical and aerial maps to make that first day your last day of the season?

The Plan 8

D ave opened the door to the camp and looked outside into the darkness while Rick and I scrambled about getting our gear together. "How cold is it?" asked Don as he cracked a dozen eggs into a skillet. "Not bad," replied Dave, "it's about 38 degrees and still damp from yesterday's rain. It should be quiet walking this morning, at least for a while. The wind is gusting a bit and is still out of the north, so I don't think this storm is quite over with yet. Better pack your Gore-Tex just in case."

It was two hours before first light, and none of us had yet to make up our minds where we were going to hunt that morning. One by one, Rick, Don, and I eventually stuck our heads out the door to see for ourselves and to mull over our options. A north wind definitely worked against Don's favorite stand along the gully, but it wouldn't slow Rick down a bit, as he was planning on pussyfooting through an overgrown field. He would just have to circle around first to get the wind in his favor before he could start his still-hunt. If the wind held steady, he might just catch a buck in his bed.

If you are not seeing deer, it may be because you are stepping afield without a plan in mind. For example, it may mean paddling a canoe to the far side of the swamp in order to get the wind in your favor.

"I think I'm going to take that stand in the corner of the planted pine plantation," chimed in Dave after we finished breakfast. "I'll bet a buck or two hid out from the storm there, and if I can sneak in before first light, I might just catch one slipping in to feed under that lone apple tree."

Don looked out the door once more and then sat down. "You know, if this storm is about over, I'll bet there will be some activity in the big block of woods. There were plenty of acorns on the ground before the storm hit, and I'll bet the wind knocked down even more. I think I'll hang my climber near the corner of the woods where that hedgerow meets the old logging road. The wind should be perfect there. Where are you going, Bill?"

"Well, since Rick is going to still-hunt through all that wet goldenrod," I said with feigned jealousy, "I think I'll sneak down into that hollow on the lee side of the hill behind the cow farm for a half-hour or so. There's a scrape line there, and I might just catch a glimpse of the buck that made it. He should be around freshening those scrapes if the storm has indeed ended. I'll see you guys back here at noon, though. It's Don's turn to make lunch, and I'll be looking forward to a hot plate of spaghetti to go along with my fresh deer liver."

If I recall right, we all saw deer that morning, but not because we stumbled across them by accident. No, we saw deer because we each had a plan to help us deal with the weather, ground conditions, wind direction, and a host of other factors that influence deer behavior. Indeed, if you are not seeing deer, then I'll bet it is due, at least in part, to not having a plan for each day's hunt. Here's a list of factors my hunting buddies and I deem important to any day afield. It is not a complete list. After all, we all don't hunt alike, but it is a starting point, especially if you are a still-hunter.

WIND DIRECTION

Wind direction is usually the number one concern of bowhunters and gun hunters alike. It is important because it dictates the direction from which you should approach your hunting area. You don't want to spook any bucks from their beds or from early morning/late afternoon travel routes with your scent. Of course, knowing the wind direction helps determine the still-hunting routes available to you. You want the wind to favor your still-hunting route and not blow in the direction from which you expect a buck to come.

WIND VELOCITY

Most still-hunters prefer a steady low-velocity breeze. On the other hand, a calm day or a day with no wind at all tends to let your human scent build up around you, and if you are moving super slowly, this pool could alert a passing whitetail. Calm days, however, are great days to use a rattle bag or grunt tube because the sound travels farther. Of course, any undesirable noises—

slamming your truck's door or loud talking—can be heard a long way, too, and can ruin your hunt.

Days of high wind velocities often spook deer, and it is not unusual to find deer feeding out in the open at odd hours of the day when the wind is blowing hard. Of course, your ability to hear approaching deer on dry leaves is greatly diminished on such days, just as their ability to hear your rattling or grunting renditions is diminished. These are great days, however, to sneak along inside a cornfield, or in and out of a buck's bedding area. Bucks like to bed out of the wind, so search for them on the lee sides of hills and in pockets of thick cover.

Your primary concern on any given day of still-hunting should be the wind.

The worst wind is one that swirls and constantly changes direction. This makes it difficult to still-hunt because you can easily be detected by a sudden change in wind direction. Unless you are rifle hunting along a power line or gas line right-of-way, these are good days to stay in camp and catch up on your sleep.

AIR TEMPERATURE

Obviously, knowing the outside air temperature helps you dress appropriately so you can you stay comfortable while you are sneaking around a brush lot. However, it is the sudden change in air temperature that I find more interesting. An unexpected drop in temperature is thought by many to trigger a flurry of rutting activity; it almost always indicates a cold front moving across the region. Colder temperatures will certainly get deer up and feeding earlier than usual, if not all day, especially in the late season.

An overnight frost is also of interest. Frozen leaves are difficult to walk on quietly, making it mandatory that you take extra time or choose an alternate still-hunting route. Under these circumstances, it is best to wait an hour or so for the morning sun to melt the frost because it gives you about an hour of wet ground to still-hunt on, or at least until the sun dries the leaves. A frost will also knock apples, acorns, beechnuts, etc. to the ground, which will eventually attract deer.

Deer generally change travel routes due to a sudden lack of cover. Be aware that although deer are easier to see when the leaves are down, the deer can more easily pick you off, too, as is the case here.

LEAF DROP

One of the most frequently asked questions in an early-season bow camp is, "Where did all the deer go?" Well, if you want to know the truth, the deer are still nearby. They may have moved around a bit to take advantage of a new food source, such as a grove of fresh acorns or beechnuts, but there is also another, less obvious reason. Let me explain.

A series of frosts, heavy rainstorms, and high winds all help knock dead leaves to the ground, including the leaves from saplings, grapevines, sumac, dogwood, etc. It is these "low-bush" leaves that deer often rely on most to give them cover as they travel about. So, with the leaves down comes a change in travel routes between bedding and feeding grounds. To answer the question "Where did all the deer go?" is simple. If unmolested, deer have changed travel routes due to the sudden lack of cover or the sudden availability of new food sources.

Keep in mind that although you can see further into the forest once the leaves have fallen, so can the deer. This goes for still-hunters as well as tree-stand hunters who must make sure leaf drop has not helped to silhouette them against the open sky.

Finally, if you are a bowhunter who prefers to hunt from ground zero, leaf drop also signifies a need to change camouflage patterns. It is time to consider wearing pants that match the fallen leaves on the forest floor with a coat and hat that match what is growing above the forest floor. This can be a deadly combo.

CLOUD COVER

Overnight cloud cover helps prevent heat from radiating off into space. Thus, morning air temperatures are generally similar to evening air temperatures. Of more importance perhaps is the fact that the moon is blocked on these nights, lowering the possibility of deer feeding heavily after sunset. On cloudless, moonlit nights deer are known to feed heavily all night long only to bed down well before sunrise.

On heavily overcast days, you'll often find that bucks will be early to leave their bedding areas in the evening and late getting back to their bedding areas in the morning, giving you an extra 10 minutes or so to catch a nocturnal buck flatfooted during legal shooting hours. Of course, on a bright day, deer have difficulty seeing into the sun, which can be yet another factor in choosing a particular still-hunting route.

SNOW COVER

There is usually an air of excitement in deer camp whenever there is snow in the forecast. Indeed, the season's first snowfall often finds deer out of tune

The season's first snowstorm seems to fool deer for a day or so into believing they are still well camouflaged.

TRACK 'EM DOWN!

I was pooped. It was the last weekend of the early bow season near my home in upstate New York and the weather had turned downright nasty. A storm front had hit hard during the night, ushering in strong winds and a 4-inch snowfall that now blanketed the entire hillside above the farm. I sat in the cab of my 4×4 with the engine running and windshield wipers on frantic, contemplating the storm and wondering if I really wanted to venture into the teeth of the tempest. A second cup of coffee did nothing to my disposition except remind me how cold it had become. Winter had indeed arrived early.

I thought back to a period early in the season when I had several opportunities at racked bucks, but I had either been caught off-balance by a buck's prying eyes or had simply blown the shot. One buck in particular haunted my memory banks. It was a modest eight-pointer that had squirted out in front of me as he trailed a hot doe across an overgrown field. My shot had gone awry, the sharp four-bladed head slicing through the top of the buck's neck rather than puncturing his vitals.

The blood trail at first looked promising, but it soon petered out along an old logging road. I eventually found my shaft down the trail, and after spending the entire morning crisscrossing the hillside, I was satisfied the wound was only superficial and would undoubtedly heal quickly.

A sudden gust of wind buffeted the cab of my Ford and brought me back to reality. The bow season was almost over, so I gathered up my strength, grabbed my bow, and exited the truck. I was soon gliding over the snow towards an abandoned pasture that often harbored deer during a storm. Almost immediately I cut a fresh set of large tracks that paralleled a hedgerow connecting the hardwood ridges above the farm to the old pasture.

Only a rutting buck would be up and about on an afternoon like this, I reasoned, so I began to still-hunt alongside the trail. The deer slowed down as soon as he entered heavy cover and then began weaving back and forth through the brush—looking for does, I thought—so I kept one eye on the tracks and the other on the cover up ahead.

Soon I came upon three fresh beds in the snow, probably a doe and twin fawns. At first I thought I might have jumped these deer, but upon

Sexing a set of deer tracks in the snow is in most cases just common sense.

closer examination, I could see that the buck had trailed each deer for a short distance until he was sure each was not near estrus. He then left the trio and continued on with his search. I was positive now I was trailing a buck, and suddenly the cold air swirling snow was of no concern.

The buck led me through the pasture and then into a thick woodlot where other does were known to bed on occasion before circling back and crossing an open field. The fresh falling snow told me I was only a few minutes behind the rutting buck, but could I actually catch up to him for a shot? I had tried this maneuver several times in past seasons, but each time the buck had caught me flatfooted and vamoosed before I could nock an arrow. Maybe today would be different.

Fresh snow and the rut helped me track this buck down.

The buck was now zigzagging through the goldenrod. I decided the only way I was going to get the drop on him was to zigzag through the goldenrod, too, and hopefully catch him off-guard before he got back into the thick stuff. The buck must have zigged when I zagged, for suddenly there he was—25 yards distant with a clump of goldenrod hanging from his mouth. I immediately withdrew an arrow from my bow quiver, dropped to one knee, and in one fluid motion picked a spot and eased into full draw. The buck looked over at me but it was too late, as the four-bladed head was already en route.

Today I probably would not have taken the shot, as the buck was slightly quartering into me, but the sharp head still did the job, severing a major artery near the kidney. Upon impact, the buck scrambled for safety by running through a nearby patch of alders. I could follow the buck's forward progress by listening to the "tic-tic-tic" of the aluminum shaft as it tapped each passing sapling. Then all was quiet.

The snow was falling fast now, so I wasted no time in picking up the blood trail. It looked like someone with a gallon can of red paint marked the buck's passing! I soon found him piled up a short distance away where he died on his feet from rapid blood loss.

Later, as I caped out the buck, I got the surprise of my life. There was a four-bladed wound on the dorsal side of his neck that was almost completely healed, save for a small yellowish puss sack. It was the same eight-point buck I had arrowed earlier in the season! He had indeed survived my first attempt but had ultimately fallen victim to an early-season snowstorm and his desire to procreate. ■

with what is going on. It takes a day or two for them to realize that their brown coats are a dead giveaway against a white background!

Snow not only lets you see deer easier, it also lets you follow their tracks. This can lead to hitherto unknown feeding and bedding areas as well as to the deer itself—if you are a skilled woodsman. The best tracking snow begins with a heavy rainstorm that soaks the sticks, twigs, and leaves found on the forest floor. This is followed by two to six inches of light snow.

A crusted snow usually spells bad news for the still-hunter. Deer can hear you approaching from a hundred or more yards away. Of course, if you are moving slowly through the woods, you can hear deer coming from a long way away. If the crust is exceptionally thick, coyotes and other predators can easily run on top while deer break through, making them easy to catch.

HEAVY STORMS

Deer usually hole up in extremely bad weather—that is, storms that last two or more days in a row. You will find them bedded down in heavy swamps, thick stands of evergreens, and on the lee side of hills and knolls. If you like to sneak and peek about, this can be an excellent time to catch a buck in his bed.

Deer will stay put until the storm abates, but as soon as it does, they will be up and about feeding, no matter what time of day. This is truly one of the best times to be still-hunting.

PREVIOUS SIGHTINGS

Knowing the general whereabouts of a buck can go a long way towards you getting a crack at him. But just because you saw him crossing a stream or working the edge of an alfalfa lot one morning does not mean you will see him again there

An advantage we still-hunters have over stand hunters is that we become quickly aware of any changes in the deer woods. Knowing that bucks have changed their feeding location, for example, can help you better plan the day's still-hunt.

If a buck is spotted acting goofy during the peak of the rut, don't leave the area. Keep still-hunting back and forth. He has probably cornered an estrous doe and will be with her for around three days.

tomorrow. In fact, it is highly unlikely you will see that buck in the same place at the same time two days in a row *unless* he is with a doe during the peak of the rut. In that case, you should make every effort to return to the exact location where you saw that deer. He has probably cornered that doe, and he will stay with her for up to three days or as long as she stays in estrous. Even if you tag that buck, someone else should still-hunt into that area and wait it out. That hot doe will attract more than one amorous buck.

STAGE OF THE RUT

Every factor to this point is influenced in some degree by the rut. For example, some buck vocalizations work best just prior to the rut while others are best used once the rut is fully underway. Indeed, a single contact grunt may arouse the curiosity of an early-season buck and help bring him into bow range, but a tending buck grunt will more than likely spook that same buck simply because the rut is still several weeks away.

As you can see, weather conditions can greatly affect deer activity, and when coupled with fresh rut sign, they should help dictate your still-hunting plans for the day. Otherwise, you step afield only half-cocked!

9 Calling on the Prowl

Bleats, blats, grunts, and the grinding of bone can all help you become a trusted member of the forest community.

I had him on a string! I first saw the buck working the oak flats below me a half-hour or so after sunup. But by the time I spotted him, he had already turned and was slipping out of sight behind a veil of leafless saplings. Instinct told me that in a moment or two he would cross the creek and disappear from my life forever if I didn't do something and do it now.

I immediately pulled a variable grunt tube from inside my jacket and imitated a rutting buck by emitting a series of three short "urps" through the reed. Suddenly, the buck turned and began walking stiff-legged towards me with his eyes searching the hillside above him for the source of the call.

I hunkered down and watched as the buck continued scanning the woods. After a moment or two, he flicked his tail left to right and then cautiously took a few more steps forward, intent on pinpointing the whereabouts of the other buck.

That's when I made a fatal mistake. Instead of waiting to see what would happen next—after all, it was the buck's next move—I raised the grunt tube back to my mouth and called again. This time, the buck swiveled his head a few degrees and looked right at me a mere 40 yards away. Although he couldn't see me crouched low behind a log, he could see that there wasn't another deer, buck, or doe on the hillside. Suspicious now, he slowly turned and eased back down the hill. The last time I saw him he was crossing the creek and, as I suspected, out of my life forever.

That long-ago episode taught me three important lessons about calling whitetails. One, grunt tubes can work miracles. Two, once a buck has responded to your rendition, don't call again until he turns to walk away. And three, where you call from is as important as the vocalization you are trying to imitate.

Today I'd be lost without a couple of grunt tubes stuffed into my pockets. In fact, I would rather step afield without my hunting knife than leave my deer calls home. That's because they give me the edge when dealing with finicky

If a buck responds to your vocalization, don't call again until he turns to walk away.

whitetails. In fact, they can turn an unproductive morning into a memorable one simply by using the right call at the right time and at the right place.

Now, most bowhunters hunt from treestands, and a call here can deliver a passing buck into bow range as well as pull unseen bucks out of the brush and into a pre-set shooting lane. But what many bowhunters don't realize is that their various deer renditions would work even better if they would call on the prowl. Why? For starters, you see more deer!

Look at it this way. You can glass an agricultural field at prime time and maybe see a dozen deer enter the opening. But if you can move about and glass several fields during that same half to two-hour primetime period, your odds of seeing dozens of deer are much better.

In addition to seeing more deer, another advantage to calling on the prowl is that you can better imitate a buck from ground zero than you can 10 or 15

Food is the key to locating early-season bucks, and a fawn bleat is one of the vocalizations that can help lure him in close.

feet up a tree. Let's face it. Bucks don't hide in the treetops, and if you are calling or rattling from any place other than flat on the ground, you can alert a mature buck that something is amiss.

You can also call from more than one position when you're at ground zero, something you can't do perched high in a tree. When imitating a rutting buck tending a hot doe, for example, it is best to move slowly along, calling every few yards. To call from a stationary position is simply not as natural. When a buck is tending a doe, he is generally hot on her heels as she moves about. This scenario is very difficult to imitate when calling from a treestand.

EARLY SEASON

Food is the key to locating racked deer during the early season. The life of a buck is simple now, and often quite pre-dictable. They basically remain bedded during the midday, feeding only in the late afternoon and early morning hours.

One option is to still-hunt along downwind or crosswind of a known feeding area at first light, blind calling for bucks as they exit the open feeding areas.

I like to stop every 50 to 100 yards next to a fallen tree or other bit of cover and wait for things to quiet down. Moderately toned buck contact grunts, doe con-tact grunts, and fawn bleats can all tweak a buck's curiosity, causing a buck to come over to investigate.

Start each rendition out softly, in case there is a buck feeding nearby. If you call too loudly, a nearby buck will likely vamoose in a hurry. Of course, have an arrow nocked before you begin calling. It is surprising how quickly an undisturbed buck can materialize in front of you!

As the sun rises, I slowly work my way downwind of proven exit trails in the hopes of catching any stragglers before they bed down for the day. Look for topographical features that promote deer travel, such as creek beds and gentle slopes that lead uphill to preferred bedding areas.

Early-season bucks can be nocturnal if they are under undue pressure. Prowling along a bedding area just before dark can be productive, however. A moderately-toned buck contact grunt might convince a bedded buck an intruder has invaded his turf, forcing him to expose himself early to investigate. Using a rattle bag, light rattling, with no antler crashing or foot stomping, might also lure a buck into the open during legal shooting hours.

PRE-RUT

The season's first scrapes herald the onset of the pre-rut. They appear rather suddenly and often in locations you found them last year. Look for scrapes

Calling along a scrape line is a killer technique during the pre-rut. Look for this season's scrape lines to appear in the same places as last fall.

along logging roads and natural funnels as well as the edges of fields and swamps. Bucks will be leaving bedding areas earlier in the afternoon and returning to their safety zones later in the morning for one reason: they are on the prowl for the season's first estrous does.

Scrape lines are my favorite locations during the pre-rut. They are only hot for a week to ten days, however, so you have to hunt them as soon as possible. The secret is to read the ancillary sign found nearby, such as tracks, scat, rubs, and the direction the forest duff is kicked, in order to determine when the buck is most likely to return.

An evening scrape line, for instance, will often have the duff kicked back towards a thicket or other bedding area. The shiny sides of any nearby rubs will also be facing the bedding area. Some scrape lines are short, with less than a half-dozen scrapes, while others can be much longer and have more than one buck working the line. I like to prowl the scrape line in the evening, ending up near the edge of the suspected bedding area by nightfall.

I will stop quite often next to a stump, rock, blow-down, or large tree to call, using mostly estrous doe bleats or fawn bleats coupled with two to four tending buck grunts. For a bit of realism, use a single-purpose call coupled with a variable tube to sound like two distinct deer. I've easily tagged a half-dozen or more bucks in this manner.

Rutting bucks will linger around feeding areas preferred by family groups of does and fawns, a prime location for a fawn bleat followed by a doe bleat or two.

PEAK RUT

There is no doubt that the peak of the rut is the most exciting time to be afield with a grunt tube. Bucks are running back and forth across the countryside all day long in their almost endless search for a doe in heat. Indeed, wide-racked "mystery" bucks, bucks we have never seen before, seem to pop out of nowhere, astonish us with their headgear, and then disappear back into the underbrush never to be seen again.

You will know the rut has kicked in when you see bucks lingering well after sunrise around feeding areas preferred by family groups of does and fawns. They will be searching for does by scent-checking the edges of openings and by staring off into thick wooded areas for several moments at a time. This is a good time to give a roving buck what he is expecting to find—a family group of does and fawns. He will quickly zero in on a couple of fawn bleats followed by a doe bleat or two.

Keep your eyes and ears open, but don't be afraid to blind call every 15 minutes or so, either. This is where a snort-wheeze vocalization can work wonders. It imitates a buck frustrated because a hot doe won't stand still for breeding. Your rendition of a buck clicking, the sounds a buck makes just prior to actual breeding, followed by an estrous doe bleat may also bring a roving buck into bow range.

Where you call from is often the key to success. Look for hedgerows, barbed-wire fence lines, dry creek beds, and terrain features such as ravines and fingers of brush that fun-

Call periodically along fence lines and other natural travel routes. Glass for that telltale white throat patch.

nel deer in and out of these feeding areas. The trick is to sneak along using available cover, stopping every 50 to 100 yards to call. Get into the habit of glassing nearby cover for a white throat patch, eye rings, or swiveling ears at each stop. Rutting bucks will often stand still in thick cover, waiting for an estrous doe to saunter past. If you can see him first, your chances of successfully calling him to within bow range with just a couple of estrous doe bleats are actually quite good.

If you catch a lone buck passing by just out of range, you can spice up your calling efforts by pushing a sapling back and forth as if it were being rubbed by a frustrated buck. This visual cue may push him over the edge, triggering him into immediate action.

Finally, pulling a focused buck away from an estrous doe can be a chore. A lost fawn bleat or, in desperation, even a fawn-in-distress rendition may tweak the doe's maternal instincts and bring her to you, with that buck in tow.

RATTLE BAGS AND RATTLE BOXES

Rattling horns have been around for quite a few years now, and used properly, they have accounted for thousands of punched tags. Indeed, there is hardly a buck hunter out there who, once having tasted success, would even think about leaving his horns in the pickup once buck season opens. Nonetheless, since their acceptance as a genuine buck-hunting tool, there have probably been more big-buck opportunities lost each season simply because those horns were taken into the woods in the first place. That's a brash statement, but once you hear what I have to say, I dare say you might agree with me.

The number one problem with real rattling horns is that they are so clumsy to carry around. Big and bulky, there seems to be no easy way to tote them back and forth from the deer woods. They do not fit easily into a backpack or fanny pack, and if you elect to stuff them inside your jacket, you stand the chance of driving a tine or two into your chest in the event you fall. Even if you tie both beams together with a cord and sling one side over your back and the other over your shoulder, one beam always seems to be in the way. There is just no easy way to pack rattling horns!

The second problem with natural rattling horns is that they make too much unwanted noise. Sure, the clashing of real bone is hard to beat in the deer woods, but all too often, we inadvertently bang the antlers together while walking or simply holding them in our hands. I fear this unwanted clicking and scraping has spooked more bucks back into deep cover than most of us could ever imagine.

As if the first two problems were not bad enough, the question of what to do with a set of horns after you complete a rattling rendition is also a problem. If you are rattling from the ground, you might have to suddenly drop them if a buck comes in unexpectedly. Of course, the resulting clatter could then spook that buck into the next county. The simple act of hanging the horns out of the way on a nearby branch can also be a nightmare. Even if you can do so without undo stretching, the beams tend to bang together as they twist and sway in the air, easily sending an alert buck elsewhere.

Fortunately, there is a solution. Rattle bags and rattle boxes can eliminate many of the problems associated with rattling horns. Just carrying them in and out of the woods is more pleasure than nuisance. Their light, compact size allows you to stuff them into your side cargo pockets or even a fanny pack for quick retrieval. And to keep them quiet when not in use, simply wrap each

Which is best, a real set of rattling horns or a rattle bag? It's up to you to decide.

with a large rubber band. Indeed, you can carry them noiselessly all day long without much effort.

The real beauty of these two rattling tools is that they require minimal body movement in order to create a satisfactory sound. This is a major advantage over full-size rattling horns, especially when rattling in open country where you might be seen from quite a distance or are in the thick stuff and need to pull a buck a few yards closer for a clean shot. Best of all, when your rendition is complete, you can quietly slide a rattle bag or rattle box inside an unbuttoned shirt and then grab your bow or shotgun.

Don't underestimate the importance of these features. A few years ago while bowhunting in Alberta, I was able to coax an early-season buck right into my lap using a rattle bag, and by "into my lap," I mean less than 10 yards from my crouched position. I would not have been able to bring that buck so close with a full-size set of horns, as the movement required by my hands to tickle and grind would have easily given me away.

Does this mean you can dump your old rattling racks? Absolutely not! Neither rattle bags nor rattle boxes have the range that a set of full-size rattling horns can muster. And some say that the "grinding and clashing" from the bags or boxes does not sound as authentic, either.

More importantly perhaps, rattling horns are also more versatile. With the ability to tickle, grind, and clash, they can be used to add a bit of realism to your rattling renditions. For example, you can use the base of the beams to stomp on the ground, imitating the pounding hooves of two battling bucks. Or, you can slide the curve of the beam up and down the trunk of a tree, imitating a buck making a rub. These are two big pluses for those who prefer to rattle with a full-size rack.

How to Still-Hunt a Bedding Area

Suddenly, a glint of bone caught his eye. . . .

N ormally, I would have stayed in bed that morning. The heavy rains and strong winds coupled with bursts of thunder and lightning would have certainly kept the bucks in their beds all night long. And any buck that did get up to feed would have undoubtedly returned to his bedding area well before first light.

It was the first day of bow season, however, and like Christmas morning, it only comes once a year! So I quickly dressed, and after gulping down a breakfast of toast and hot coffee, I was soon cruising down the road in my 4×4 towards a grown-over farm I had been bowhunting for nearly 15 years. Due to the inclement weather, I decided I would only take a perfect 15-yard shot at a relaxed animal. Since I knew the farm like the back of my hand, I believed I would have little difficulty locating a lung-shot buck in the heavy rain.

As I surmised, the bucks were not moving that morning. Nonetheless, I slipped around the edges of some old crop fields for over an hour in the hopes of catching a hungry buck off-guard. I saw nary a tail, though, so I decided to still-hunt my way to a specific section in an overgrown field, a section that bucks traditionally choose to bed when there is a storm front passing through.

I circled around and began sneaking crosswind through the brush-choked goldenrod field one step at a time. Suddenly, I caught the movement of a buck's rack less than 10 yards in front of me. I froze and studied the tip of bone protruding through the weeds with great care. I could soon make out the body and head position of a yearling six-pointer relaxed in his bed facing to my left and waiting out the storm.

I slowly nocked an arrow and after picking a spot, brought my bow to full draw. "Gotcha," I said to myself when the pin settled behind the buck's shoulder. "You're mine!" Satisfied I could make the shot, I let down the bow and learned a valuable lesson in the process. Bedded bucks are not invincible. In fact, if you play your hand properly, they can be quite vulnerable to attack!

LOCATING BEDDING AREAS

One of the secrets to hunting whitetail bucks successfully is pinpointing seasonal feeding areas, bedding sites, and the various types of travel routes that

Backtracking a buck's winter trail can lead you to heretofore undiscovered bedding grounds.

connect the two. It is the bedding area that is the most important, however, at least until the rut kicks into high gear. That's because his security cover is the hub of a buck's core area. Find this hub, and you can more accurately predict a buck's next move.

Although a buck can bed just about anywhere, I always begin my search by checking out the high ground first, then any large impenetrable tangle that looks too difficult for a two- or four-legged predator to easily navigate. The bigger the tangle, the bigger the buck; and the higher the peak, the older the buck.

Locating bedding areas is a year-round job, though. If you live in snow country, then you can start looking for buck bedding areas by following deer tracks in the snow. Circle known winter-feeding areas in the early morning, and then follow any large single set of tracks that lead away from the area. Invariably, they will lead you to a secret spot where that buck is spending his daylight hours. You can also backtrack a set of fresh deer tracks in the afternoon or early in the evening. Again, the trail should lead to an area where that buck bedded during daylight hours.

Heads of ravines, islands inside swamps, steep ridges above lakes and rivers, and other probable bedding areas can be easily found by studying a topographical map of your hunting grounds.

If you stumble upon several beds of varying sizes, you can bet you found a bedding area preferred by a family group of does and fawns. A mature buck usually beds alone, and his bed is considerably larger than the average deer bed found in your hunting area.

Of course, you can also follow deer trails that lead away from preferred feeding areas at other times of the year to locate a buck's bailiwick. An extra large set of tracks on a late summer exit trail may be enough to point you in the right direction. As the rut nears, fresh rubs and rub lines along with fresh scrapes and scrape lines can also direct you to a buck's stronghold.

Studying topographical maps is yet another way to locate a buck's bed-room. Those brown squiggles offer a plethora of information if you will only

Rubs and rub lines can sometimes point you in the direction of a buck's secret lair.

take the time to study their relationships with not only each other but with adjacent swamps, clear-cuts, orchards, and the like. Brad Herndon's book, *Mapping Trophy Whitetails*, is a must-read on the topic.

What does a buck's bedroom look like? Where specifically does he prefer to rest during most daylight hours? Well, it could be along the edge of a ridge, on a slight dip just below a high peak, in a flat spot in the middle of a thorn-apple thicket, at the head of a ravine, the downwind side of a block of woods, just inside a goldenrod field, alongside a stone wall, on the rim of a plateau overlooking a clear-cut, adjacent to an abandoned piece of farm machinery in an overgrown farm field, inside a hedgerow, next to a pile of stones in an otherwise open field, deep inside a cattail marsh, along a creek bed bisecting an uncut corn field, inside a finger of brush leading in or out of a swamp, in the bottom of an irrigation ditch, high on a hummock inside a swamp, alongside a blow-down, inside a blow-down, tucked close to chainsaw slashings, out in the middle of a hay mowing, or in any number of other strategic locations where a buck can hide yet take full advantage of his primary defenses to avoid detection.

Of course, last fall's rub lines and scrape lines can also point you in the right direction. Begin scouting for these soon after the snow melts in early spring. And while you are at it, look for clumps of rubs around some of the probable sites just mentioned. Keep in mind that a buck often rises from his bed in the evening, urinates, and then rubs a tree or two before striking out to a feeding area. A cluster of rubs is generally a good sign you have pinpointed a buck's bedroom.

Over the years, I have found that bucks of all ages move from one bedding area to another quite often, especially in the early season before the rut takes hold. Changes in food sources and ground cover are two good reasons for moving, as are incoming storm fronts and summer spot-lighters. Later, as fall approaches, bird hunters can move deer around, as can bowhunters who take chances with their pre-season scouting.

Outside the peak of the rut (the only time bucks and does really bed together), I think the main reason for bedding in any one particular spot has to do as much with pre-dawn prevailing winds as anything else. A buck may simply prefer to move upwind to a bedding area rather than downwind or crosswind that particular morning.

BEDROOM STRATEGIES

Hunting a deer's bedding area has always been a touchy subject, especially for bowhunters. In most areas of the country, we get first crack at the herd,

Are there times when still-hunting through a buck's bedroom makes sense? Absolutely!

and after glassing bucks all summer long, it is tough not to set up an ambush just outside a buck's security zone. At first it seems like a no-brainer, but jumping a buck from his bedroom usually results in the buck going nocturnal. Indeed, once a mature buck knows you are onto him, he usually disappears from your life forever.

That is why most experts will tell you to stay out of a buck's core area. Don't scout it, don't walk around it, and don't let the wind carry your scent to where you believe the buck is resting during daylight hours. Just stay as far away as possible. If you are going to set up on him at all, you must do so only with the utmost of caution, and then only by carefully skirting downwind along the periphery of his security cover.

This is usually good advice, but there are times during the deer season when setting up along the edge of a buck's bedding area, or even entering it, makes good sense. In fact, it could be your ace in the hole!

TIMING IS CRITICAL

When should you knock on a buck's bedroom door? If you are going to do it, you must do so in the early-season or pre-rut periods. Once the rut nears its

Windy, stormy days can muffle your approach to a buck's daytime hideout.

peak, bucks vacate their usual haunts. There's no use protecting a buck's bedroom now because he isn't home; he's out chasing girls!

You might also want to bow-hunt a buck's bedroom when the time you have left to hunt is limited, such as when your are on vacation or the season is about to end. Of course, "your" buck may have finally gone nocturnal due to your periodic intrusions, indicating your chances of seeing him again this season are nil. Indeed, if he won't come to you, then you must go to him!

Finally, you might want to sneak into his core area for the sheer challenge. If you are like me and know the whereabouts of several bedding areas, then nosing around one or two before the rut kicks in can be a ton of fun.

Weather is your only other important consideration. The best days to still-hunt a buck's bedding area are stormy, windy days. Heavy rain or snow tends to muffle noises and keep your scent near the ground. If the wind is blowing hard, the waving vegetation also serves to camouflage your forward progress.

Slip crosswind into a bedding area and you have a chance of catching a buck napping. You have virtually no chance if you head directly into the wind.

The real secret to still-hunting bedding areas is to sneak in crosswind and spend your time looking for a bedded deer—not one standing up—paying particularly close attention to blow-downs, ridge rims, and the other preferred bedding sites mentioned above for the hint of antler. A buck will move his head around a bit with every slight noise and each passing breeze, and "rack rotation" is what so often gives him away.

Keep in mind you are not going to get within bow range by working directly into the wind. If he is bedded with the wind to his back, he will probably see you coming; if he is bedded facing into the wind, he will probably hear you trying to sneak through the thick ground cover bucks love to bed up against.

If, on the other hand, you slip in crosswind and take advantage of all available cover, you have a chance of catching him lying down. He will, after all, hopefully have only one eye pointed in your direction! It is amazing how close you can actually get to a bedded buck before he comes unglued.

This is when a quality pair of binoculars comes in handy. You must glass anything and everything that even remotely looks like part of a deer. Besides the hint of antler, white muzzles, throat patches, and a single black eyeball are all dead giveaways.

This past season I was sneaking and peeking across a tall goldenrod field when I noticed something odd out of the corner of my eye along the far edge of the old farm field. At first I dismissed it as a stump, but instinct told me to check it out. I finally glassed the object, and sure enough, it was the rump of a bedded buck. He had already spotted me, however, and once eye contact

A bedded buck often betrays his hideout by shifting his head about: it's the rack you see first.

I made an easy shot after catching this yearling buck in his bed.

was made, he hightailed it into the thick brush. You must do everything right and see the buck before he sees you if you expect to get a bow shot.

Each fall I catch at least one deer napping by still-hunting, and over the years, I have managed to tag three with my bow. I have also missed a couple of easy shots (gulp!) while countless other deer have jumped out of their skin when they caught me flatfooted nearby. That's why, when conditions are right, I prefer to spend a day "sneaking and peeking" my way through a buck's bedding area. I'm not telling you it's easy, but if you get a shot, I guarantee you it will be a most exciting day afield!

11 Walking the Line

Bucks will freshen scrapes and scrape lines soon after a storm passes.

Something told me I should have turned around and gone back to camp right then and there, but I didn't. It had been raining on and off since first light, and by noontime I was both hungry and soaked to the skin. Nonetheless, the conditions were perfect for still-hunting, so I continued to walk away from the logging road and up the spur towards the crest of the ridge.

I hadn't gone another hundred yards before I heard it coming. First one drop and then another, and soon rain pelted the forest with such ferocity it was nearly impossible to hear anything above the roar of the storm. I quickly took refuge beneath the boughs of a mature spruce tree and watched in amazement as sheets of wind and water ravaged the landscape. Huge branches broke and crashed to the ground while thousands of autumn leaves swirled past me like so many yellow pinwheels gone berserk. I pulled my hooded sweatshirt up over my head and then leaned up against the trunk of the tree. I had no choice now but to stay put and tough out the storm.

The buck had also sensed the change in air pressure and bedded in a thicket of mixed spruce and fir a full ten minutes before the tempest hit. There he closed his eyes for a few seconds at a time and waited for the thunderclouds to pass on down the valley. Eventually, the winds subsided and the heavy rains gave way to sprinkles and light drizzle. When the dark clouds disappeared over the horizon, the buck rose from his hideaway, urinated, and then peered intently along the top of the ridge for three or four minutes. Satisfied all was safe, he vigorously shook the rainwater from his coat like a dog after a bath. He then took a few steps forward and browsed momentarily on some fallen leaves before he, too, worked his way along the spur.

Normally, the ten-pointer would have waited for the cover of darkness before moving along that natural passageway that led down from the beech ridges and into the clear-cut below. However, the urgings of the rut were still somewhat powerful, and the buck had other things on his mind besides food. He had left a line of thirty or so scrapes along that spur, and now that the storm had passed, it was again time to check up on each one of them.

In farm country, bucks routinely parallel fence lines, irrigation ditches, and old stone walls.

The five-and-a-half-year-old buck, now lean from the rigors of the rut, was working his way downhill along that scrape line when he brushed up against the trunk of a fir tree. A dead branch, protected from the heavy rains, snapped loudly, alerting me to the big buck's presence. I leaned up against a beech tree and looked up the trail. Suddenly, I could see a wide but short-tined buck a mere 25 yards away, plodding his way directly towards me. I had no time to move to a better shooting position, or even wipe the water droplets off my scope. In fact, I dared not even breathe as I slowly swung the barrel around the tree and placed the crosshairs squarely between the buck's ears— the only available shot. The sight picture was an "×" instead of a "+", but the 180-grain silvertip from my ought-six was true nonetheless.

For a second or two, I thought I had only stunned the big deer, for although his body fell directly to the ground, his head was still held high above the forest floor. I quickly learned, however, that the short-tined ten-pointer's G-2 had pierced a standing deadfall, and this was what was holding the buck's head aloft. I later paced off the shooting distance—22 feet! It was my closest whitetail to date with a rifle, and one of the heaviest, tipping the scales back at camp the next morning at 220 dressed pounds even.

There's no doubt that whitetail bucks are line walkers. Rub lines and scrape lines are two obvious examples, but bucks also walk parallel to man-made objects such as overgrown hedgerows, dilapidated stone walls, barbed-wire fences, drainage ditches, and logging roads. In more natural settings, you can find bucks sneaking along less-defined lines such as riverbanks and the edges of crop fields. Indeed, you can always find a buck walking one line or another. The trick is to be still-hunting along that line at the right time. Let me explain.

EDGES

Locating a "line" in the big woods can be difficult, unless you look for edges. An edge is where two or more habitat types come together. Although whitetails can utilize the whole forest, they prefer those edges or "ecotones" where browse and grazing forage can be found adjacent to thick heavy cover. If you glass the big woods from an open hilltop, these edges are sometimes readily apparent. In fact, you can easily eliminate 90 percent of the forest and narrow down your search for wilderness bucks by simply zeroing in on an ecotone.

Indeed, good edge occurs naturally. Look for deer sign around old beaver dams, thick swamps, brush-choked ravines, alder-lined creeks, high water lines, and seasonal ponds. In addition, always be on the lookout for that magical line that separates hardwoods from a stand of softwoods. Wind-storms, forest fires, and avalanches also create edge habitat and are worth

Power lines and other rights-of-way produce miles of edge, attracting bucks much like a clear-cut.

exploring within a year or two of their birth, especially if adequate security cover is nearby.

Man, as he so often does, interferes with the natural order of things, and in the process creates edge habitat desired by deer. Old quarries, gravel pits, and controlled burns immediately come to mind, as do abandoned railroad beds, gas pipelines, underground communication cables, and, of course, overhead power lines.

All totaled, logging practices, especially the various types of clear-cutting, and overhead power lines create the most acres of manmade edge. Given a choice, start scouting three- to ten-year-old cuts that are formed in long thin strips—especially if thick tangles of shelter-type cover are growing nearby. This pattern, similar to the swaths carved out for overhead power lines, has proven to be a better wildlife attractor than square or circular-shaped clear-cuts.

Each of these edges begs to be worked over by a careful still-hunter. One of the best edges I ever found was in east-central New Brunswick. Try to picture this scenario: To the east, a 12-mile-long beech ridge that abuts a valley of mixed conifers. The edge that occurs naturally here would be hot by and of itself, but logging operations left a series of clear-cuts in the valley that are now super buck feedlots. The spot to be is in the northeast corner of one of these clear-cuts, where the beech ridge and clear-cut meet a square-mile block of thick, uncut spruce-fir. Three edges of prime big-buck habitat! Indeed, I've tagged two wilderness bucks here over the years that dressed out over 200 pounds.

EARLY SEASON

Food is the key to locating bucks during the latter days of summer, and in farm country, that means active agriculture, such as bean fields, alfalfa lots, and especially uncut cornfields. The mistake many still-hunters make hunting cornfields is that they sneak 100 yards or so off into the woods in hope of intercepting a buck on his way to the field. The best location for a still-hunter, however, is right along the edge of the field. Bucks that bed in the corn, as well as those that enter the field from any one of a myriad of locations, usually end up "walking the line" around the field one or two rows in from the edge. This strategy is good for at least as long as the corn remains standing, and longer if the cornfield butts up against a block of woods, swamp, or other type of heavy cover.

You can also key in on rub lines to pinpoint the whereabouts of a late summer buck. The good news is that mature bucks usually make the first rub

Bucks will patrol the outside rows of a standing cornfield, a hot route for the still-hunter.

lines of the year, and they are a dead giveaway to one of those buck's preferred travel routes. Since most woods are not crawling with mature bucks, however, these early-season rub lines can be hard to find. Your job will be easier if you know the whereabouts of one of last year's early-season rub lines. If that buck is still alive, chances are you will find his fresh rubs near that old rub line.

Keep in mind that in hilly terrain, mature bucks usually bed high and feed low. Thus, the shiny side of their rubs will usually be facing uphill for an evening rub line and downhill for a morning rub line. Once in a while, an older buck will bed low in a swamp or creek bottom and feed high on the year's first acorn, beech, or hickory crop. In these cases, the shiny sides of the rubs will be reversed.

The problem with all early-season rub lines, though, is just that. They work best before the rut begins. Once scrapes and scrape lines pop into view, the early-season rub lines begin to lose their effectiveness.

Examine the ancillary sign surrounding a scrape line to unravel the size of the buck and when he is likely to return.

PRE-RUT

Scrape lines have probably accounted for more mature bucks on the meat pole than any other line in the woods. Why? A scrape line offers you a plethora of information about the buck that created it. Indeed, if a hunter takes the time to study all the auxiliary sign in addition to each scrape in the line, he can often deduce the size of the buck and the quality of his rack by studying the tine marks in the scrape. Common sense should then tell you his line of travel and the direction from which he came.

For example, the buck's line of travel can easily be determined by adding up all the available sign. Start by noting the direction the forest duff was tossed from the scrape site, the direction any hoof prints, the side of the sapling where you found the buck rub, and the natural lay of the land. Examine any nearby trails and then follow your instincts. The next scrape shouldn't be too far down the line.

If you are familiar with the terrain, you should now be able to figure out from where the buck came and when he was last present. For example, you know that a scrape line that exits a bean field along a deer trail was probably made early in the morning right after the buck spent part of the night in the field feeding or looking for does. Likewise, a line of scrapes found just inside the woods and parallel to the edge of that same feedlot was probably made just before dark when the buck scent-checked the bean field for does.

Knowing when the buck is most likely to return to his scrape line is crucial because you want to meet him there the very next time he visits. In the above two scenarios, for example, a morning still-hunt downwind of the exit trail may be your best bet, while still-hunting in the evening downwind of the second scrape line could earn you a shot at that other lovesick buck. Sometimes a buck working a scrape line needs a little coaxing. A combination of estrous doe bleats and tending buck grunts can be a deadly one-two punch on a lovesick buck.

A rub line will often delineate the path rutting bucks take as they travel from one doe bedding area to the next in their seemingly endless search for an estrous doe.

PEAK OF THE RUT

Once the breeding season kicks into high gear, buck movements seem impossible to predict. Indeed, one morning a buck can be seen chasing does around a hayfield, and then that afternoon that same buck will be seen a half-mile away scent-checking bedded does in an old apple orchard.

Nonetheless, rutting bucks still like to walk the line. When a buck hooks up with an estrous doe, he will stay with her, breeding her several times over a three-day period. Then he strikes out in search of another hot doe by making a beeline to the next known family grouping of does and fawns.

Prior to the rut, this buck could have easily pushed 275 pounds on the hoof. Still, these two outfitters have all they can do to load him onto an ATV. I rifled him at 22 feet.

The route he takes may lead him across wooded hillsides, down the edge of a steep ravine, or along that invisible line that separates hardwoods and softwoods in the big woods, but in each case, there is often a rub line to guide him to his destination. Like the early-season rub lines, breeding rub lines can be hard to locate. If you know your hunting grounds like the back of your hand, however, the line is quite obvious: it is the most direct route available. In fact, there will be fresh tracks visible on that trail, a trail that is used *only* during the peak of the rut.

The trick now is to still-hunt this rub line, again on the downwind side. This can be especially productive when you have nearby feeding areas and bedding zones preferred by family groups of does and fawns located on posted property. When a buck exits these posted hot spots, the trail he takes could very well be along a breeding rub line on your property.

Another tip: A breeding rub line often runs alongside a fence line, irrigation ditch, or a hedgerow. If you have your heart set on a better-than-average buck, look for breeding rub lines to be a mixture of fresh rubs and old gray rubs. Why? They are a good indication the same buck has been working that line for several years, increasing his chances of sporting a trophy rack.

12 Still-Hunting the Peak of the Rut

A buck's behavior changes radically with the approach of peak rut. To get a shot, you must adjust your hunting methods accordingly.

I have said it before and I will state it here again: without a doubt, still-hunting whitetail bucks is one of the toughest ways to punch a tag. Not only are a buck's senses of smell and hearing more acute than ours, his sense of sight has evolved into a veritable radar detector when it comes to moving objects. All it takes is one false move, one unnecessary head-bob, and the buck of a lifetime will vanish without a trace.

Indeed, still-hunting is nerve wracking, but it is also the most rewarding of all the deer hunting methods, especially during the rut when bucks are suddenly up and about all day long searching out and then breeding receptive does. They accomplish this task in a surprisingly efficient and systematic manner, but a buck's behavior changes radically with the onset of the breeding season, and to get a shot, you must modify your early-season and pre-rut still-hunting routines. That's because a rutting buck no longer beds in the same tangle, feeds on the same ridge, or travels between the two in a predictable fashion, and unless scrapes, scrape lines, and rub lines are located in areas frequented by does, you are not likely to see him there, either. Indeed, you are just as likely to see a buck in one valley as the next once the does start coming into estrus.

To help pinpoint those magical days, including the peak of the rut, you can consult with a local biologist, but too many factors beyond their control prohibit them from giving you more than a general range of dates. You are much better off spending as many days afield in a row as possible and then relying on your daily observations to determine when the bucks you hunt have actually begun breeding does.

Here are a few indicators to key in on. The first change you'll notice as the rut nears, if you are still still-hunting along traditional travel routes between bedding and feeding grounds, is a reduction in the number of buck sightings. You'll wonder if there are any bucks at all left in your hunting area. Rest assured they are still in the vicinity; they have just switched their priorities towards breeding. Indeed, a group of yearlings lingering uncharacteristically in the open late in the morning or early in the evening is good sign the rut is heating up.

Another indication the rut is upon you is the presence of running deer tracks in the wood lots. You may even see deer running short distances, as if you jumped them from their daytime beds. The fact is you probably didn't jump them at all. Horny bucks, checking on the breeding status of those bedded does, will often get them up and running during daylight hours. And even if you don't actually witness these early attempts at love, the deep, splayed tracks you find on the hillsides betray the event.

Of course, any bucks you do spot will not seem as wary, appearing instead to be on a mission of sorts. And that they are! Their attentions are now devoted to seeking out the season's first estrous does, and they go about this by sniffing well-used trails and by staring into brush-choked ravines, grassy plateaus, and other pockets of cover known to harbor family groups of does and fawns.

With the breeding frenzy just around the corner, it is time for you to shift gears and pay closer attention to these changes in buck behavior. Bucks have only one thing on their mind now—sex—and although an individual buck is not as predictable as he was during the pre-rut, bucks in general are now more vulnerable to the careful still-hunter.

Once the rut kicks in, there is no excuse for slipping back to camp after a couple of hours afield for a snack and a short nap. You must pack a lunch and hunt from sunup to sundown. After all, Old Mossy Horns could step into view at any time of the day, and if you are not out there looking for him, you're simply not going to get him!

Looking for a rutting buck? Find the does by still-hunting along the edges of those feeding locations does now prefer.

DOE FEEDING AREAS

During the rut, I often position myself downwind of a major food source known to be frequented by does at pink light. Then as the day dawns, I move slowly along the edges glassing for bucks. I not only spot them in the thick stuff but also in the wide open as they check out those does that are still in the fields. In farm country, cut corn lots are my favorite, but apple orchards, meadows adjacent to swamps, and CRP fields overlooking active agriculture are excellent choices, too.

Don't be afraid to zigzag your way back and forth through the nearby cover all morning, or at least as long as you continue to see deer. A lovesick buck has no plans to bed down at first light, and there's no telling when you might spot him. I've had bucks walk up behind me on my third pass around a cornfield in as many hours.

Another early-morning strategy is to still-hunt creek beds, hedgerows, and overgrown pastures that funnel deer in and out of the feeding areas. Bucks will sometimes push estrous does into these conduits at first light, and if you play the wind right, you can walk right up behind them.

The hottest spot near feeding areas is often a steep ravine, and if it is choked with scrapes and scrape lines, so much the better. Although a buck no longer needs his scrapes once he hooks up with a doe, the best scrapes and scrape lines are laid out in areas naturally frequented by many does. While other scrape lines are abandoned, those near active agriculture demand a second look-see during the rut.

DOE TRAVEL LANES

When the morning sun warms the frost-covered fields, it's time to circle around and check out the trails leading to known bedding areas frequented by does. You can still-hunt along the downwind side of these trails if you like, but a much better tactic is to work your way slowly across these exit trails at right angles.

If you look carefully, you may find a rub line or a barely visible trail that when followed seems to take advantage of terrain features and available cover. This is the path a rutting buck will take as he searches the area for an estrous doe, and this is the route you should take as you still-hunt for that buck.

Keep the wind in mind. That buck may be traveling crosswind or quartering into the wind to scent-check the moving air as well as the exit trails for estrous does. And go slowly. It is not unusual to spot a buck standing as still as a statue as he stares down one of those trails. Bucks use their eyes and ears to locate hot does, too!

Start paying more attention to the routes does take as they travel between their bedding areas and preferred feeding locations.

Still-hunt in and around a doe bedding area at first light and you may bump into a rutting buck. This tactic is especially deadly after a cold front has passed through the region. Estrous doe bleats are one of the calls of choice.

DOE BEDDING AREAS

Once the does bed, it's time to cruise the periphery of their bedding grounds. But don't jump them if you can help it; family groups of does, yearlings, and fawns are the best bait a still-hunter can have right now, and you want them to remain put.

I like to sneak and peek around doe bedding areas early in the morning, especially at first light and especially right after a cold front has passed. Bucks that can't find a suitable doe around feeding areas will soon be poking around one bedding area after another in their seemingly endless search for a doe in heat.

If you see does popping out of the brush lots and weed tangles at any time of the day, you can bet a buck is working the area over, looking hard for a hot doe. This is not the time to be timid, but one of the best times to go right in after him. Play the wind and don't worry about making too much noise. In fact, any noise you do make may actually attract that buck to you. He may just think you area an escaping doe, or even another buck trying to horn in on the action.

Eventually, you will begin to see unfamiliar bucks in the open at midday, and then bucks actually breeding does. Now is the time to check out those out-of-the-way locations you wouldn't be caught dead still-hunting earlier in the season because of the relative absence of deer and deer sign. These hide-outs are now safe havens for bucks traveling with a hot doe. When pressured by subordinate bucks, a mature buck will often push an estrous doe here to bed and breed, if he is lucky, in solitude.

In areas of high deer concentrations, that buck would probably not be so lucky. I've seen as many as nine bucks bedded in the immediate vicinity of one diminutive doe. As soon as one of the yearling bucks got too close to the doe, the mature buck would roll his eyes back and lower his head in a threatening manner. Generally, this is not a good situation for a still-hunter, but on this particular occasion, I was able to put the sneak on one of the bedded bucks. The 180-pound eight-pointer I tagged that day never knew what hit him.

CONNECTING ROUTES

A buck will follow a hot doe for maybe three days, feeding sparingly when she feeds and lying down nearby wherever she beds, be it in an open goldenrod field or along a hedgerow. Then after breeding her several times, he is off in search of another liaison. Bedding areas are now hot all day long, even if the weather is nasty. Indeed, bucks will weave in and out one doe's bedroom after another all day long until they come across another willing doe.

During the rut, connecting routes between bedding areas are another still-hunting option for you to ponder. The trails are often faint, but now that you know the whereabouts of bedding areas, these trails are easy to find. When you exit one bedding area, just take the most direct and energy-saving path to the next. They will lead you along hedgerows, fence lines, and across open fields—places you wouldn't think about still-hunting bucks at any other time of the year because of the lack of cover.

IN HOT PURSUIT

During any day afield, you will have bucks pass by you just out of range. Some will be alone looking for a doe in heat while others will be bird-dogging a doe already in heat. Some will even pass by your blind side unnoticed. Whatever the circumstances, your ace-in-the-hole

How can you lure a buck away from a hot doe? Try a fawn or doe bleat. It might just bring the doe to you—with the rutting buck in tow!

while still-hunting the peak of the rut is a grunt tube. A tending buck grunt or a doe bleat may be all it takes to turn a wandering buck's head, but what can you do when you find a buck hot on the heels of an estrous doe? Is it possible to lure that lovesick buck in close enough for a shot?

Generally, you have two chances of pulling a rutting buck away from a hot doe and into your sights: slim and none, and slim just left camp. At least that is what I was led to believe for many seasons, until I began paying closer attention to the chase phase of the whitetail rut. Today, I look forward to the days when I can locate a buck chasing a doe around and around because I know with a little luck and the right timing I can entice that buck into bow range.

The first time I tried such a stunt ended in failure. I watched a diminutive doe, with her tail at half-mast, slowly pick her way across an overgrown farm field with a 140-class behemoth hopping along behind her. The buck looked over his shoulder in my direction when I let out a few deeply toned tending grunts, but he then continued on behind the doe. I then tried scraping an aluminum arrow shaft up and down the metal riser of my bow. Although the buck and doe seemed interested, they both soon disappeared into a thicket, never to be seen again.

Since then, I have learned that tending buck grunts and rattling rarely turn a buck around when he is in close proximity to a doe near estrus. In fact, it often causes the buck to horn the doe away from the intruder and into a more secluded area. What buck wants competition at a time like this?

However, what will turn a buck around is a fawn bleat or a doe bleat. No, the buck is not interested in checking out another female, but the doe might very well be. A doe contact call, for example, will alert her to the fact that another deer is in the vicinity, whereas a fawn bleat might very well appeal to her maternal instincts. Today I don't hesitate to aim a call or two at the hot doe. Indeed, if you can turn the hot doe around, the buck will surely follow.

But what do you do when there is more than one buck in hot pursuit? What about those times when the doe has momentarily given the buck the slip? Well, rattling is generally still not the tactic of choice, but the right notes from a grunt tube will more often than not lure that buck right into your lap. Let me explain.

During the chase phase of the rut, bucks use sight, sound, and smell to help them keep track of a hot doe. If she is not yet ready to breed, she will often seek the thickest cover available in order to elude her amorous suitors. This makes the job all the tougher for the bucks.

A lost buck will now go nuts trying to relocate that hot doe. He might go to her last known location to try and sniff his way back to her, or he may stand still on a high point in an effort to see where she is hiding.

Your job now is to help him out. A doe-in-heat bleat will surely call the buck towards you, but so will a tending buck grunt. You want the target buck to think one of his competitors is hot on the heels of his love interest. In many cases, this will cause him to throw caution to the wind and walk right towards you.

I said earlier that rattling does not generally work during the chase phase. But you can take one-half of your rattling horns and vigorously rub a nearby sapling. During the rut, bucks often make several frustration rubs when a hot doe is still not yet ready to stand and breed. Hopefully, the target buck will get the message and come prancing over for a look-see.

In fact, almost *any* sound will cause a lost buck to think the doe or a competitor is over in your direction. I have called bucks in by simply tossing stones down a hillside and by breaking a few branches with my feet. Even the twang from a strand of barbed wire, which imitates a deer jumping over a fence, is enough to bring a lost buck into range.

If you spot the buck, but he is

One doe near estrus can attract several bucks, any one of which may become "lost" as the doe scrambles about in an effort to lose her tormentors. These bucks are actually quite vulnerable now to the right vocalization as they too scramble about in an effort to relocate that hot doe.

too far away to hear your grunt tube, your antler rubbing, or any one of a number of unorthodox sounds, you have one last option. You must only use this during the bow season and only on property where you have exclusive hunting rights. A white handkerchief slowly waved side to side once or twice from a position deep in cover imitates the "flag" of a doe in heat and should instantly grab a lost buck's attention. And don't waive it vigorously up and down, either, as this signifies danger. Rutting bucks are suckers for all kinds of sex tricks, but they are not stupid. Any sight, sound, or smell that spells trouble is enough to knock some sense into him, which in turn will only cause the buck to seek deep cover elsewhere.

Whatever strategy you choose, one thing is for certain. The chase phase of the rut can offer you a splendid chance at calling in a rutting buck.

FOUR SPECIALTY CALLS

Yearling buck grunts, doe bleats, doe-in-heat bleats, moderately toned buck grunts, fawn bleats, buck contact grunts, yearling buck tending grunts, and even fawn-in-distress bleats are all proven deer calls. Each fall, knowledgeable hunters who know how to imitate these vocalizations in the wild tag thousands of whitetail deer.

Yet sometimes big bucks give these same good hunters the slip precisely because these very calls are used. If you spend enough time in the deer woods,

The deep guttural tones of a mature buck tending a hot doe will attract a mature buck, but younger bucks will shy away.

you will eventually be confronted with a situation where the old standbys are not as effective. In fact, in some cases, these basic calls may even be detrimental in your pursuit of a racked buck. Why? Because at that moment one the following four specialization calls would be more appropriate.

Tending Trophy Buck Grunt

Take the tending grunts of a three-and-a-half-year-old or older buck as an example. Deep and guttural, they reflect the sexual urgency of a mature big-bodied buck. This vocalization certainly stirs the imagination, and it sells a lot of grunt tubes in discount stores each fall. Unfortunately, when used in heavily hunted regions, this call will often scare away yearling and two-and-a-half-year-old bucks. As a result, many knowledgeable hunters refrain from using the tending grunts of a trophy buck when hunting in such an area.

However, therein lies the rub. When still-hunting wilderness regions

A mature buck "clicks" as he is about to breed a hot doe. Mimic this vocalization to bring a passing buck into easy gun or bow range.

where wide-racked bucks die of old age without ever seeing or smelling a human being, the tending grunts of a mature buck do indeed attract trophy bucks, in part because there are simply higher numbers of older bucks present in the population.

One of my strategies when still-hunting big woods areas like the Adirondacks is to call blind during the pre-rut when bucks are still highly territorial. How? By periodically emitting a series of evenly spaced, staccato-like tending grunts of a mature trophy buck. Sure, a younger grunt or even a doe-in-heat bleat might bring a big-racked mature buck out of his daytime bedding area to investigate, but the deep vocalizations of another big buck is more likely to succeed.

Buck Clicking

Here is another case in point when a specialization call can be more effective than a standard vocalization. When a buck is in the company of an estrous doe near the very peak of her cycle, he will often make a clicking noise just moments prior to copulation. It sounds much like someone dragging a thumbnail across the teeth of a plastic comb, one tooth at a time. You can speed up or slow down the clicking, and you can increase or decrease the duration of each episode, but each individual click is separate and distinct.

When the rut is in full swing, this clicking will signify to a passing mature buck that a hot doe is somewhere nearby and that mating is about to take place. Using a moderately toned or high-pitched series of clicking, a sexually experienced trophy buck just might believe that a younger and less mature buck is about to breed and rush in to take over the breeding rites. A doe-in-heat bleat or the tending grunts of a yearling buck might also work, as might a fawn bleat, but the clicking of a young buck adds a sense of urgency to the equation.

Snort-Wheeze

A snort-wheeze is made by a buck exhaling air through his nose in a very specific cadence. Once you have heard it, you won't forget it. It occurs when two

A snort-wheeze will at times pull a rutting buck away from a hot doe.

bucks of similar status suddenly encounter each other, especially around a food source, and serves as a warning to the intruder buck to back off or there will be a fight.

The second time it occurs is when a buck that is tending a hot doe is suddenly confronted by another buck trying to horn in on the action. Again, the snort-wheeze serves as a warning.

And finally, you will sometimes hear a buck make a loud snort-wheeze when a hot doe refuses to stand still long enough to allow breeding to take place. The buck is undoubtedly warning the doe to stand still—or else!

Once while still-hunting with archery tackle, I had a 150-class twelve-pointer snort-wheeze at me twenty times or so, thinking I was an intruder buck. I brought him into bow range but was unable to get a shot due to thick brush. Even so, it was an electrifying experience!

Bucks growl at does when they do not stand still to be bred. It can be a killer call when bucks are on the prowl during the breeding season.

Although hunters have long reported the snort-wheeze, it has only been recently that a snort-wheeze deer call has been made commercially available. It seems to work best during the peak of the rut when mature bucks are tending does. Your rendition of a snort-wheeze, either alone or added to a tending buck grunt or an estrous doe bleat, may be all it takes to pull a mature buck away from a hot doe. But be prepared; like the buck I just mentioned, he will come in looking for a fight!

Growl At 'Em!

I may have very well saved the best for last. Yet another whitetail vocalization has been discovered and caught on videotape. We have probably all heard it at one time or another but failed to recognize its significance. Bucks have been caught actually growling at each other or at an estrous doe. That's right, growling! As with other deer vocalizations, you have to listen for it to hear it. But like the tending grunts of a mature buck, buck clicking, and the snort-wheeze, it is a memorable sound not easily mistaken for any other vocalization.

The Buck Growl is a unique and exciting new call developed by the Drury brothers. "It is a very emotional call," says Mark Drury, "and represents the fact that there is estrus in the air. It is beyond a grunt, however. It is a loud, loud bawling grunt sound made by a mature buck that is impatiently waiting for a doe that he has been tending to finally stand and breed. When a buck hears another buck growl, he is coming to your tree.

"We know that growling works by its lonesome," adds Drury. "But it also works in conjunction with other vocalizations, especially tending buck grunts, the snort-wheeze, or even rattling. Used with these other techniques, an imitation buck growl can give the impression that there are several bucks dogging a hot doe, as they so often do during the chase phase."

None of these calls works all the time, but they work often enough that every still-hunter should pack one or two whenever he is afield during the peak of the rut. Indeed, still-hunting trophy-class whitetail bucks is a difficult task. A deer call may be all the edge you need to turn the odds in your favor.

PART III
Still-Hunting Tactics for Bowhunters

Advanced Bowhunting Skills 13

I caught some movement out of the corner of my eye and froze in mid-step until I could figure out what was going on. Slowly, I turned my head until I could see an eight-pointer with good eye guards, probably a yearling animal, working his way towards me across an old pasture. I decided right then and there to take him if an opportunity presented itself, but first I would have to close the distance.

It appeared the buck would enter the woods along an abandoned logging trail that bisected the wood lot. I would need to move forward about 15 yards in order to take a shot—not an easy task in the dry leaves that littered the forest floor that morning. As luck would have it, however, a strong breeze fueled by the rising morning sun stripped more dry leaves off the standing oaks. The rustling easily covered my forward progress.

Head down, the buck was less than 30 yards away and moving closer. It was now or never, so without taking my eyes off of him, I slowly and methodically pulled an

Pennsylvania buck hunter Scott Staines nailed this Iowa beauty from ground zero. The buck wasn't even remotely aware of his presence in part because Staines saw the buck first and reacted accordingly.

Many treestand hunters are surprised when they come eyeball to eyeball with a whitetail. The experience sometimes creates a convert.

arrow from my quiver, nocked it, and dropped to one knee. The buck, feeding nonchalantly on fallen mast, had no idea I was crouched nearby. When he finally stepped into a small hole in the brush, I picked a spot and in one fluid motion brought my bow to full draw. After holding my top pin behind his shoulder for a brief second, I released a vaned shaft at his vitals. The deer bucked his hind legs like a rodeo horse upon impact and sped off along the cart road with his tail tucked tightly between his legs. His efforts to escape were to no avail, as I soon found the buck piled up less than 100 yards away with a perfect lung shot.

Many archers begin their still-hunting careers as they sneak to and from their treestands knowing full well that their odds of connecting on a whitetail buck will soar if they can get in and out of their stands undetected. Sooner or later they have a close encounter with a deer, and for some that is all it takes to hook them on still-hunting. They quickly realize, however, that to consistently score from ground zero they have to develop some special bowhunting skills.

UNORTHODOX SHOOTING POSITIONS

Most bowhunters practice at known yardages either in the backyard or at the clubhouse. They stand facing or quartering into a bull's-eye target and shoot one arrow after the next from 15 to 40 or so yards night after night until they are slapping shafts into tight groups at those distances.

Then the real enthusiasts climb onto a garage roof or into a treestand and shoot some more from known yardages in an effort to replicate a probable shooting scenario. Foam bucks add a bit of realism to the sessions, and by the time the bow season rolls around, the confidence levels of these bowhunters are sky high.

If you want to be a successful still-hunter, however, these shooting sessions accomplish little more than help you establish good shooting form and dialing in your pins. In fact, they can do more harm than good. For starters, you rarely know the exact shooting distance when still-hunting whitetails because things happen so fast in the deer woods. One minute you have a buck at 40 yards and then suddenly he is at 28 yards—and closing. And secondly, you rarely get to shoot at a deer from a standing position. Only a few of my bow-bagged deer tested my shooting skills past 30 yards, and only a couple of those were taken from a standing position.

So how should a still-hunter practice? The secret is to practice shooting in the deer woods from unknown yardages across uneven terrain. First you will

Do you want to be a dead shot in the deer woods? Then you need to practice shooting from unorthodox positions over broken terrain.

learn how to cant the bow when shooting along hillsides and how to compensate for those acute uphill and downhill opportunities. You will soon realize that you may have to kneel down to thread an arrow through the brush, or bend over at the waist and duck your head before you can come to full draw. You may even have to shoot sitting down with your back up against a tree trunk or you may have to come to full draw while lying on your stomach, and then rise to one knee in order to take the shot.

My friends and I will often wander through the woods or around a bow course taking turns choosing a challenging shot from an unknown distance. Stumps, leaves, patches of mud, and 3-D deer targets are all fair game. The rules are simple: no more than one arrow per person at a target and no shots can be taken from the standing position.

During these practice sessions you may notice that you do not always come to full draw. And even if you do come to full draw, your bowstring might be striking your arm or wrist on a regular basis. When I witness a practice session where a bowhunter sometimes misses by a country mile or experiences episodic poor arrow flight, I immediately suspect he is not coming to full draw in part because his draw length is a bit too long. A worn serving or a scuffed arm guard usually confirms my suspicions.

Over the years I learned to solve these accuracy problems by shortening my draw length an inch and a half to 28½ inches. Now when I bring my Mathews to full draw from a contorted shooting position, I ease it right back to the "wall," leaving no guesswork as to whether I am at full draw or not. Indeed, creeping—especially with the single cam but also with traditional equipment—can cause even the best-aimed arrow to go awry.

The shorter draw also keeps my elbow "cocked and ready to rock," helping to eliminate wrist slap, which is more likely to occur when shooting from odd angles. It may feel a bit awkward at first, but it will pay big dividends, especially when you have to shoot through a small hole in the brush from a kneeling or stooped-over position. In fact, with this kind of practice, it doesn't take long to be transformed from a mere target archer into a still-hunter who is a crack shot with his bow and arrow.

YARDAGE ESTIMATION

As you may have already guessed, the second skill you need to develop is estimating the distance of the shot. "Most bowhunters target practice only from known distances, beginning at 15 or 20 yards and then working their way out to 40 or even 50 yards," says taxidermist Rick Plant from Rochester, New York. "Although this may help them to sight in their bows, it generally leaves them with a false sense of readiness when it comes time to take a shot, a problem that is compounded when they must shoot from an unorthodox

Keep your shooting eye honed during the season by setting a foam target out in the woods at unknown yardages.

position. That is because we often do not know the exact yardage when the moment of truth presents itself."

Stump shooting and 3-D tournaments can help you sharpen your yardage estimation skills. So can a range finder, especially if you use it as a reinforcement tool. Simply eyeball the shooting distance before checking your estimate against the read out on the range finder. You should see improvement during your first practice session.

Be aware, however. Do not make the mistake many bowhunters do when guessing yardages at 3-D shoots and stump-shooting contests. If you are going to shoot from an unorthodox position, like kneeling or sitting down, then you must guess the shooting distance from that position—not standing up. Things look mighty different when you are at or below eye level to any big game animal.

You must also be cautious when shooting uphill or downhill at acute angles. The distance "as the crow flies" either downhill or uphill may be 30 yards, but the actual shooting distance will be far less. In this regard, the more acute the angle, the shorter the actual shooting distance. The rule of thumb is to guess the distance as if the animal is on the same plane as you. If the animal is standing downhill next to a tree, do not estimate the distance to the tree's trunk, but rather to a point on that tree that is perpendicular to your position. If you are thinking about taking an uphill shot, then you will have to look into the hill and imagine where that animal would be standing if there were no hill present. In both cases, animals standing uphill and downhill from you are really closer than they appear.

Keep in mind that you rarely have an opportunity to put a rangefinder on a big game animal before the shot. Rutting whitetails have a habit of showing up unannounced and when you least expect them.

A buck I arrowed in New York can serve as a case in point. I was still-hunting through an abandoned farm late one October morning when I decided to turn around and walk back to my waiting 4x4. My mind was on breakfast when suddenly a doe came rushing past me through the goldenrod with a nice buck in hot pursuit.

I had only a few precious seconds to estimate the yardage, come to full draw, and shoot. Fortunately, I practice estimating distances from a kneeling position on various size 3-D target animals during the off-season, and I was able to accurately judge the shooting distance to that buck. The buck bolted upon impact but collapsed less than 100 yards away, leaving me utterly flabbergasted at the quick turn of events.

A rangefinder makes a good teaching tool, but rarely does a still-hunter have time to use one during those moments leading up to the shot.

Another problem associated with your "realistic" practice sessions is shooting lanes. Most lanes are cleared at the clubhouse, but in the hunting world, weeds, leaves, and brush can sometimes interfere with broadhead flight and accuracy. We all know that a twig can easily send a vaned or feathered shaft off into the wild blue yonder, but do you know what effect goldenrod has on arrow flight? What about a cluster of oak leaves?

You will soon learn that the closer the weeds or leaves are to the deer the less effect it has on accuracy or broadhead flight. I have shot several deer partially concealed by leaves or goldenrod stems, but I would never take a shot when the buck is standing in thick brush unless I knew I could thread a broadhead through the branches. This is where your yardage estimation skills play another pivotal role.

The trick here is to arc your arrow's shaft past a protruding branch, and the way you do that is by "pinning" the offending branch. For example, let's say you have a rutting buck at 35 yards, but an overhanging branch 20 yards in front of you seems to be blocking the shot. Put your 20-yard pin just above or below the branch, and then look to see if your 35-yard pin offers you ample clearance. If it does, let her rip!

TIMING IS EVERYTHING

You can't expect to down a deer or any other big game animal if you do not shoot, but being a dead shot means being a responsible shot. There is no honor in wounding and then losing an animal because you elected to take a Hail Mary shot rather than wait for a closer shot or a better angle.

Recently while still-hunting in Kansas, I played hide-and-seek with a 150-class eight-pointer. I had him dead to rights at 40 yards, but as is so often the case, the buck turned around and walked through a chest-high patch of brush. There was no way I could thread an arrow through that tangle, so I let him pass despite his trophy status. If I had shot and just wounded him, I probably would never see him again. But I might still get a shot at him in the future since I passed on that low-percentage opportunity.

Knowing when to shoot and when to pass is a learned trait, based on experience and time spent afield. This is where your target buddies lose out. As mentioned earlier, the best bowhunters I know spend most of their free time in the woods looking for deer and deer sign. Their goal is to locate ambush zones where they can take shots at animals well within their effective accuracy range. Not just any shots mind you, but high-percentage shots. They know when to release an arrow because they have done their homework by studying the anatomy and behavior of the big game animals they pursue. Then when the season opens and they find a buck in front of them, they know that if things don't happen to work out on this particular animal, another buck

The more quality time you spend in the woods looking for deer and deer sign the better the hunter you will become.

will come along and take his place. They don't panic, thinking the deer in front of them is the only deer in the woods or it's the last one they will ever have in shooting range. Indeed, all is not lost, as sooner or later the opportunity they are looking for will present itself. There is no need to take risky shots or shots well beyond your capability.

DITCH THE RELEASE

Oh, I can hear the moans already. "I can't give up my shooting release! I can shoot dimes with it at 30 yards!"

Well, it is true that on average a run-of-the-mill release shooter is far more accurate than a good finger shooter—at the target range. But when it comes to shooting deer from ground zero, a release is more like an albatross around your neck. It simply gets in the way of everything you need to do! Let me explain.

Those who bowhunt from treestands can leave their release attached to the bowstring while they wait for a buck to saunter by. Even if they don't, they are high enough off the ground that the movement associated with attaching a release is unlikely to be seen by the buck.

But that same release can spell trouble for the still-hunter. For starters, you cannot walk through the deer woods with an arrow nocked. Not only is it not safe, it is difficult to maneuver through the brush with a razor-tipped arrow sticking out in front of you like some sort of Roman spear. It simply snags on every sapling, grass stalk, and weed, eventually dulling the cutting edges to the sharpness of a common butter knife.

Secondly, the attachment process itself involves excess hand movements, a dead giveaway to a buck standing only a few yards away. To make matters worse, some release models snap onto the bowstring. If the buck did not bolt when he caught you fumbling with your release, that snapping noise at close range is sure to send him hightailing it over the nearest ridge.

Most bowhunters use a mechanical release these days. Releases do not, however, offer any advantages to the still-hunter. In fact, they are generally a hindrance.

The most damaging case against still-hunting with a mechanical release, however, is the time it takes you to attach it to your bowstring, and time is something you don't always have when you suddenly find yourself eyeball-to-eyeball with a rutting buck. And once that release is attached, it can be difficult to make any last-minute adjustments, something that is sometimes necessary as the moment of truth nears.

On the other hand, shooting with fingers is quick, quiet, and involves far less motion. The best part is that I have never left my fingers behind in the truck, and I have never lost a finger in the woods even though I do fall down

Learn to shoot with fingers and your chances of getting a shot at close range will skyrocket. Why? You can come to full draw with a minimum of movement.

on occasion. Fingers never need adjustment, they never malfunction, and they are low maintenance. Best of all, perhaps, is that they have been with me since birth and have, therefore, cost me nothing. Unlike a lost or defective release, replacing a bruised or broken finger is a problem, however, and may be the only drawback to not using a mechanical release.

One fall just before the bow season opener my friends and I were roaming through a 3-D course practicing on deer targets at unknown yardages when one of my pals slipped in the mud, sending his release high into the air. We all saw it sail through the air and watched it hit the leaf-strewn ground before us. After we stopped laughing, and despite all our efforts, we were aghast when we could not find that release! If we were hunting, that would have ended the hunt for our friend right then and there.

As you can see, still-hunting requires you to think and act differently than our treestand brethren, and to learn a critical new set of shooting skills. Indeed, everything is more difficult when you go eye-to-eye with a whitetail buck at ground zero. Everything.

The Moment of Truth **14**

The opportunity came as expected, and I pulled the shot off without a hitch. It was the third day of the New York big game season, and I was quite excited about the prospects of arrowing an early-season whitetail. I had been still-hunting uphill and into the wind when I spotted the buck first, a fine seven-pointer, as he fed cautiously downhill through a stand of mature oak. His wide rack glistened in the late October light as he periodically lowered his head to scoop up the fallen mast. The nut crop was spotty that year, but this particular twenty-acre grove was loaded, and deer from the entire hillside came here to gorge themselves on the sweet acorns.

I focused my Zeiss 8×30 binoculars and took a long hard look at the sleek buck. His rack extended well past his ears, and his 180-pound frame seemed to be in prime condition. I decided then and there to take him. He was only 40 yards away, but I needed to get closer—much closer. As it turned out, I almost got too close.

The buck fed broadside to me as I moved slowly through the fallen leaves with hopes of halving the distance between us, when for some unknown

A rutting buck can appear anytime, anyplace, giving you precious little time to prepare yourself mentally for the challenge. This is where experience and extra time in the woods can pay big dividends.

reason the buck turned and fed towards me. I could easily hear him feeding now as he vacuumed up the oblong morsels and crunched then again and again with his back molars.

I immediately dropped to one knee, nocked an arrow, and came to full draw as the big whitetail passed behind the trunk of a fallen oak. He kept coming and at three yards it was either shoot him or risk being gored by those bobbing antlers. The decision to shoot was easy. I picked a spot just behind his left shoulder blade, and when the buck turned slightly to his right, I released a razor-tipped camo shaft. The broadhead struck with a resounding whack, almost taking the buck off his feet. He bolted then, back uphill and out of sight with scarcely a twitch or wasted motion. I tilted my head and cupped an ear to get a general direction of travel before sitting down on a log to catch my breath and wait things out.

The buck was down, but first a heavy shower and then the evening's darkness foiled my attempts at a quick recovery. I telephoned Gideon Hanggi, the local game warden, fired up a Coleman lantern, and after an incredible 600-yard blood trail, we found my buck piled up inside a goldenrod field.

GROUND ZERO
Coming to full draw is the definitive moment in still-hunting. Indeed, there is nothing more exciting than being eyeball-to-eyeball with a mature whitetail

All the scouting and practice sessions in the back yard will be brought to bear when it's finally time to bend the bow on a live deer. Will you be ready?

This is no time to second-guess yourself. Either you are ready, or you are not.

buck and knowing you have the drop on him. Even an archer who has tagged a dozen deer from a tree stand will stammer a bit when he tells you that he nearly stepped on a buck that morning after climbing down from his perch. And you can tell from his enthusiasm that the encounter will live in his heart forever.

But getting close to a buck from ground zero is what it is all about for a still-hunter. In fact, it is the only way you are going to realistically get a shot. Your goal is to find yourself so close to an unsuspecting buck that you can feel his heat. That's when time will seem to stand still as you meticulously prepare yourself for the upcoming shot.

It is also a time fraught with difficulty. Even if the wind is in your favor, you still have the buck's eyes and ears to worry about. Drawing down on a buck standing less than 20 yards away is no easy task. He is, after all, the master of his domain.

There is a secret to making the shot. And when I tell you what it is, you are going to hit yourself in the forehead with the heel of your hand and say, "Of course, why didn't I think of that!" But before you can contemplate coming to full draw, you must be completely camouflaged, especially your face, eyelids, ear, neck, and hands, as outlined in the opening chapter. Uncovered, you are not only easier to see, but the pronounced presence of these features will uncloak you as a predator.

I am reminded of the release from wildlife artist Jack Paluh depicting two eastern woodland Indians putting the sneak on a pair of fighting whitetail bucks. In *Disguised Approach*, each Indian has the rack and cape of a buck draped over his head and shoulders, which effectively distorts their appearance—and their intentions. I am not advocating using deerskins and cast antlers as part of your camouflage, as that could be risky in this day and age.

Getting an arrow out of the quiver and onto your bowstring can be a nerve-racking experience. A lot of opportunities are lost because the buck catches the movement or hears the arrow ricochet off the hood of the quiver, the sight bracket, or metal riser.

What I am saying is that you need to take great care in disguising your human form.

Full camouflage is only half the answer. You must also learn to take advantage of terrain features and available ground cover. In fact, relying on these features must become second nature to you. Do not walk boldly across an opening; stick to the shadows and skirt the edges. And do not walk on the flat of a ridge but rather just below the crest. In both of these cases, you want to see what is ahead of you without being seen yourself.

When in doubt about what path to follow, pretend there is a bedded buck just ahead. Then think about how you can sneak up on him without the buck seeing you. If you must pussyfoot along the edge of the swamp, then use the alders as cover. If you must step into the creek to mask your forward progress, then do so without sloshing.

Staying out of sight, and being quiet about it, will go a long way towards getting you a close encounter with a buck. In those places of moderate deer densities, like the farm country in the Midwest and along the eastern seaboard, I can count on having one close encounter for every five

Yearling bucks are the bread and butter of the still-hunter, especially in heavily hunted states in the Northeast and Midwest. I shot this one at around 10 yards. Notice the billed cap and two-tone camouflage.

days afield. But getting close solves only half the problem. You still have to get the shot.

So, what is the secret? The very first thing I do when I catch an undisturbed buck flat-footed is immediately drop to one knee, and if I can do so next to a log, a tree trunk, or a bush, then so much the better. My goal is to mask my human form. No longer am I a two-legged creature standing nearly six feet off the ground, a creature deer seem to instinctively fear. Instead, I am a dark stump, a bush, or a mound of earth. I am part of the forest primeval—and nothing more.

The next thing I do, without taking my eyes off exactly where I want to shoot the deer for more than a second, is to nock an arrow. Only a fool still-hunts with a nocked broadhead, so you must extract and nock an arrow without banging the shaft against the hood of the quiver or slapping it against the sight bracket or riser of the bow.

I then wait patiently and motionless until I can come to full draw without alerting the buck to my presence. This is where timing is crucial. Even if he catches you making the move, the buck will often hesitate a second or two before he bolts, simply because he doesn't know what you are. And a second is all it takes to skewer a whitetail. After all, you look more like a stump than a wild-eyed predator, and that is all the edge you need to make the perfect shot.

Of course, do not come to full draw when he is looking in your direction, but rather avoid eye contact by wearing a cap with a visor and slowly lowering your chin. You can also hide behind the bow limbs and riser while waiting for the buck to turn his head, step behind a tree trunk, or look the other way. You will be surprised what you can get away with when you take your time and think things through carefully.

I have had lots of deer over the years step to within 10 yards of my crouched position and not see me. The closest I ever had a buck pass by was within a single yard. I surmise he simply never expected a human being to be kneeling so close to him in the goldenrod! To this day I wished I had reached out and slapped his butt, but there was a bigger buck nearby and I didn't want to alert him to my whereabouts. If I was standing tall and motionless that evening, I doubt that buck would have been fooled. Indeed, it is times like these that make still-hunting so much fun.

Bowhunting Thin Cover

15

I had the place all to myself. I stood tall on an old tree stump that morning and glassed across the three-year-old clear-cut with care. Piles of brush, rotting logs, briars, stands of goldenrod, an old apple tree or two, plus dozens of treetops left behind by the buzz saw provided more than ample cover for the fifteen to twenty deer I knew frequented the hillside. Satisfied the coast was clear, I eased forward along a cluttered logging road, stopping periodically to glass brush-choked ravines and to listen for the tending grunts of a rutting buck.

By mid-morning, I had seen three does and a tall-tined eight-pointer that passed by just out of range with his nose to the ground like an old hound dog. However, I didn't tag a buck that particular Saturday. In fact, I never nocked an arrow. But over the years, I have dragged a couple of good bucks from this clear-cut, including a fat eight-pointer that was in hot pursuit of an estrous doe and a two-and-a-half-year-old nine-pointer I arrowed in his bed.

Why do I consistently have this whitetail hotspot all to myself? That's easy. Other bowhunters shun the area because there isn't a tree suitable for

Bucks will often seek out thin cover simply because bowhunters avoid the area. Why? There is no place for a treestand!

139

Bucks love brush lots adjacent to open fields. If you are careful, you might even catch one napping.

a treestand anywhere in sight. Indeed, most bowhunters erroneously believe that although there are plenty of whitetails to be found in goldenrod fields, thorn-apple thickets, cattail marshes, overgrown farm fields, pastures, prairie lands, clear-cuts, and other types of thin-cover habitat, hunting them from the ground with archery tackle is an exercise in futility.

Well, nothing could be farther from the truth. My favorite tactic for bowhunting whitetails in thin cover is to still-hunt, and I find that still-hunting is often the strategy of choice when bowhunting clear-cuts and abandoned farmlands for racked deer.

The best places to still-hunt are the transitional zones adjacent to large openings. These are magnets for big bucks, especially during the rut when bucks seem to follow estrous does about like puppy dogs on a leash. Start out at dawn by sneaking and peeking along the downwind edges of transitional zone cover. Unattached does will be leaving feeding areas soon after pink light and passing through this thin cover on their way to preferred bedding areas. It is absolutely amazing how many different bucks you can see in those first few hours of the morning as amorous bucks zigzag back and forth trying to locate an estrous doe.

They not only use their noses to locate a willing doe, as you might well expect, but their eyes and ears, too. Indeed, a buck will sometimes stand still for 10 to 20 minutes as he scans the cover for a doe. With his head erect, his white throat patch is easily visible and a dead giveaway to the sharp-eyed still-hunter. A soft doe bleat, a tending buck grunt, or a combination of both calls will most certainly get his attention.

Another tactic is to still-hunt briar-rich hay lots and thick goldenrod fields adjacent to heavy cover. These openings often have pockets of brush or uneven terrain that hold deer during the rut. Bucks will push does into these offbeat places during the peak of the breeding season in the hope of keeping the doe to themselves. In areas of high deer concentrations, though, more than one buck usually learns about the hiding place. I've arrowed a couple of bedded bucks in this type of thin cover, including a two-and-a-half-year-old eight-pointer that proved to weigh over 200 pounds on the hoof. I arrowed him at 25 yards as he lay bedded in a mixture of goldenrod and thorn apple next to an estrous doe and eight other bucks!

Still-hunting is also the strategy of choice for bowhunting standing cornfields. During the rut, bucks will scour the fields looking for estrous does, but in the early season, bucks will use the fields for food and cover. Pre-season glassing from a safe distance will help you get a handle on the local deer populations during the late summer and early fall. On-site scouting should be minimal, however, and even then, you must practice scent control. Your goal is to learn the general whereabouts of a buck or two without spooking them and then stay clear of the area until opening day.

A few years back I discovered where a buck was holed up in a posted woodlot during the heat of the day. Just before dark, he would leave his bedding area by walking along a weed patch. He would then jump a barbed-wire fence into a corn lot, which he used as a conduit to an adjacent alfalfa field. There was not a suitable tree for a treestand within several hundred yards, but once I learned his evening routine, it was an easy task to ambush him by still-hunting down between the rows before he reached the feeding area. The

Goldenrod grows tall during wet summers, providing great cover for shy bucks.

Cornfields always seem to harbor bucks. But where should you concentrate your efforts? In large fields, I zero in on the edges first before striking out for those tall trees out in the center. Bucks seem to use these trees as beacons as they navigate about the standing corn. Good location for scrapes, too.

eight-pointer ran about 100 yards before expiring after being shot in the heart from about 12 or 15 yards.

When bowhunting thin cover, you will be amazed at how little cover you actually need to hide behind when it comes time to waylay an unsuspecting buck. The trick, and I will say this many times, is to get off your feet and take your shot from a kneeling or sitting position.

SPOT AND STALK

The classic still-hunt occurs when you spot a nearby buck before he sees you, and you either nock an arrow immediately or maneuver yourself a few yards to ready yourself for the shot. But what happens when you are sneaking and peeking along and see a buck well past your shooting abilities? There is only one answer: you have to stop peeking and start sneaking!

One of the most difficult places to bowhunt whitetails is in the wide-open spaces. Here, deer can see a bowhunter sneaking along from quite a distance and can be gone before the hunter can work himself into shooting range. Indeed, a buck spotted on the rolling prairie or feeding in a hay lot or even crossing a goldenrod field is, in most cases, quite safe from a bowhunter.

Or maybe not quite so safe, for there is a chink in the whitetail's armor whenever you can catch him flatfooted and out in the open. Normally, bucks that live in wide-open spaces move little during daylight hours. However, as the rut approaches, bucks are up and about earlier in the evening and later in the morning in their efforts to keep closer tabs on family groups of does and fawns. If you can see a buck before he sees you under these circumstances, you might have a chance of tagging him. Let me explain.

The secret is to use a good pair of field glasses to follow his every move as he works himself across the open. Be aware that a buck will often appear to be feeding rather nonchalantly through thin cover before suddenly disappearing from view. Unless it dropped down into a dry creek bed or irrigation ditch, it most likely bedded down. Keep

I love doe tags! Mmm good!

You don't need much cover to hide a still-hunter. Use irrigation ditches, hay bales, land contours, and strips of uncut weeds to camouflage your forward progress. Open fields can be hotspots—if you spot the buck first.

especially vigilant when bucks get near a single tree, rock piles, and even abandoned farm machinery, as they will take advantage of any available cover to bed during daylight hours. Your job is to mark the exact spot by paying close attention to nearby vegetation and terrain features. Then, keeping the sun to your back and the wind in your favor, stalk the buck's bedding site.

Even if you get close, it doesn't mean you have him dead to rights. I once put the sneak on a bedded Pope & Young buck I first spotted some distance away on the western prairie, but when I eased my way into bow range, I couldn't tell if the buck's resting body was facing left or right. If I guessed wrong, the arrow would only end up in the ground. When the buck suddenly stood up, I overestimated the yardage—a common mistake easterners make when bowhunting areas of thin cover in the West—and sent a broadhead harmlessly over the buck's back.

As you can see, still-hunting is your best option when dealing with bucks that like to stick to thin cover. Once you are successful, you'll be wondering why it took you so long to give it a try. The best part is that you will undoubtedly have your new hotspot all to yourself. After all, there are no trees here to hang a stand!

After the Shot 16

The buck seemed less cautious than usual. Maybe it was the crisp November air or the early morning darkness. Maybe not. He trotted cross-wind along the edge of the alfalfa field, stopping often to test the wind and peer into the blackness. Normally, he would have been well on his way to a bedding area by now.

As the darkness faded, he cupped his ears forward and stared across the field. Two does had finished feeding on the alfalfa and were now entering an adjacent overgrown orchard. Again, the buck raised his snout, but the magic odor was not in the air. Not yet, anyway.

With his nose to the ground, the buck zigzagged across the alfalfa lot, stopping briefly to peer into the abandoned orchard. Although gaunt from the rigors of the search, he ignored the lush green alfalfa and continued with his mission. The odor he sought was definitely not in the valley. He turned uphill, away from the apple orchard, and onto a well-used path, adding his large set of heart-shaped prints to the trail's collection.

It was a brisk northwest wind that watered the eyes of the camouflaged bowhunter that morning, not the mask-

A hard-hit buck can still be lost if you don't pay attention to detail. Indeed, knowing what to do after the shot is as important as taking the shot itself.

145

ing scent of raw skunk juice. He slid silently past the two whitetail does in the orchard as he, too, moved up the hill and into the wind. Stopping often, he surveyed the terrain carefully before continuing his planned ascent. He knew not what lay ahead.

The buck reached the hilltop first and waded into a sea of blackberry and belly-high goldenrod. A lone white pine, its outer bark frayed from earlier rubbing, stood conspicuously on the far shore like a beacon guiding the buck into a protective cove of alder, thorn apple, and second-growth poplar.

Suddenly there was a loud crashing off to his left. Sunshine ricocheted off his hide as he swiveled his flanks to investigate, but it was only the wind thrashing the alders. I guess it was the flash of tan and brown that caught me in mid-stride. A tight-racked nine-pointer, in full rut, stepped briefly into view and then disappeared. He simply turned about and walked behind a tangle of thorn apple, or had he somehow sensed me and then shrewdly exited along a faint trail?

I stood motionless for several minutes. The nine-pointer had, in fact, bedded down and was now holding a downhill vigil, lying almost perfectly still with the wind to his back. Almost perfectly still. A pivoting head revealed his left main beam and then an ear tip and suddenly the buck's entire outline came into sharp focus. At 21 yards, I picked a spot, slowly came to full draw, and released a razor-tipped arrow. The buck bolted from his bed, but I knew

Inclement weather, bird hunters, thick brush, and a host of other factors can all wreak havoc on even the best-hit deer.

his efforts to escape would be to no avail. He left a blood trail the proverbial blind man could follow.

Indeed, blood trailing a well-hit buck should be an easy task, and although I quickly found that buck, outside influences can wreck havoc on even the best-hit deer. Radical changes in weather conditions, such as rain, snow, or heavy wind storms, can obliterate blood trails, while coyotes, wild dogs, bird hunters, and even other bowhunters can sometimes jump a mortally wounded deer, causing it to run for hundreds of yards. And if that is not enough, red leaves, thick swamps, chest-high goldenrod fields, and short dead grass can all add to the difficulties encountered while blood-trailing mortally wounded deer.

To complicate matters further, what appears to be a good hit might not be as deadly as you first surmised. A case in point: One year a friend called to say he had shot a deer in the lungs by passing an arrow right behind the front shoulder, but he couldn't find any blood. We later learned that the deer was quartering into him when he shot. Sure, the broadhead entered the buck behind the front shoulder, but due to the sharp angle, the broadhead missed the lungs and passed through the abdomen. Now instead of tracking a double-lung-shot buck, we were trailing a buck shot in the stomach.

Also keep in mind that once you release your arrow, its flight path and the buck's reaction to the shot are out of your hands. Your arrow can be deflected by an unseen branch, or the buck can flinch with your release. Even if that broadhead still strikes the deer, it can be anybody's guess what path it will take inside the body.

Another case in point: One year while still-hunting I hit a buck high in the chest while he stood broadside to my kneeling position. But instead of the arrow passing cleanly through the buck, it struck a rib and did a 90-degree turn, traveling down through his heart! However, that shaft could have easily passed through the gut instead, which would have made the blood-trailing chores all the more difficult. This is one reason why you should treat every shot as a hit, and every hit as deadly until you learn differently. That said, here are twenty-five tips to help you do just that.

BE PREPARED

Blood-trailing a bow-shot big game animal really begins before you take your first step into the deer woods, and most certainly before you release a broadhead.

Tip #1: I carry orange surveyor's tape with me when I am afield, but I also keep a gas lantern with plenty of extra mantles, a large flashlight with extra bulb and batteries, a cell phone, topo map, compass, dry clothing, and rain gear stowed in my 4x4. A couple of whistles, a pair of walkie-talkies

Orange flagging tape can not only help you stay on the blood trail, it can also help you relocate your deer should you need help later on getting it back to camp. Be sure to pick up the tape after the hunt. You don't want to tip off wandering bowhunters to your hotspot, do you?

(where legal), and a GPS system could also be useful in some circumstances.

Tip #2: If you prefer dark fletching as I do, consider attaching florescent nocks. They can help you determine the path of the arrow, pinpointing the entry point if you have a hit or the arrow's path past the deer if you miss. They are also helpful when looking for an arrow buried in the leaves.

Tip #3: Tan a deer hide and study the position of the various types of hair during the off-season. This will help you determine where the arrow entered the deer as well as where it exited. Hairs that are half black and half gray with a black tip may lead you to believe you hit high on the back, indicating a possible heart or lung hit if you were hunting along the edge of a steep ravine. But curly white guard hairs will tell you the arrow exited near the groin region, indicating you may be dealing with a paunch-shot animal instead.

Tip #4: Know where the vitals are on the animal you are pursuing. I once had an acquaintance tell me he shot a buck through one kidney, the liver, both lungs, and the heart with a single arrow. He couldn't tell me, however, why his "perfectly" shot animal traveled over a mile before expiring!

MOMENT OF TRUTH

Tip #5: Keep your eyes open. You might very well see the deer drop or change course as he tries to make good his escape. Look for evidence of a hit, such as a scruffy or discolored hide, sprays of wet blood, or an unusual gait. You might even see the arrow shaft hanging out the far side. I also mark the last spot I saw the deer in my brain,

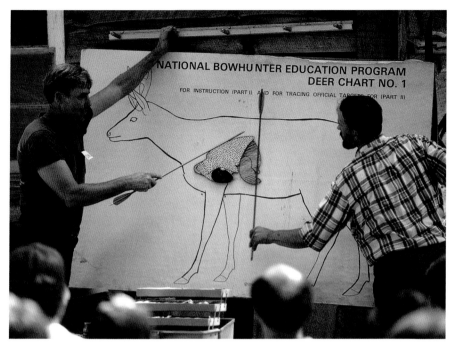

Memorize where the vitals are on a whitetail deer before you shoot, and then visualize the path the arrow might have taken after the shot.

using my binoculars if necessary. A nearby large tree, a swaying sapling, or even an old stump will suffice.

Tip #6: Listen intently for any unusual sounds. I once heard an aluminum arrow shaft go "tic-tic-tic" as the buck bolted through some brush. Not only did this outline the buck's death route, but it also told me how far the buck ran before he keeled over.

Other noises worth paying attention to include the twang of a deer jumping a barbed-wire fence, antlers hitting brush, and the splashing of water as a deer crosses a stream. Keep listening for at least 20 minutes. A liver-shot deer, for example, may lie down immediately only to get up and move away 15 minutes later. You might just hear him walking if the leaves are dry.

Of course, you may have missed, as evidenced by the thud an arrow makes when it hits a tree or the clanking of a shaft as it ricochets off rocks behind the deer. You must not be duped, however. I once heard my broadhead bury itself into a gravel bar while still-hunting caribou on the tundra. I thought I had missed a book animal, but when I watched the Boone & Crockett bull drop a few minutes later, I realized my broadhead had passed completely through his rib cage before slamming into the ground.

Listen intently after the shot and pay close attention to any noises such as water splashing or branches snapping for up to twenty minutes after the shot. Why? The death run of a wounded buck is rarely a straight line.

Tip #7: This next step is important. After the shot, mark your exact location with a long strip of surveyor's tape before you move anywhere. Or if possible, shoot another arrow into the ground. Why? You may need to return to that exact spot later to help you determine where the deer was standing when you released your broadhead. Indeed, bits of bone and a few strands of hair are hard enough to find as it is. It will also help you remember where you last saw the deer.

Tip #8: Some things you don't want to do are yell, cheer, give out a war whoop, or call your friends on your cell phone after the shot. The deer may not have associated the hit with a human being and will soon lie down. But your human voice may force him to push on deeper into the woods.

Tip #9: Even if you are sure the deer is dead, wait 20 to 30 minutes before trailing. This will give you time to calm down and better assess the hit. More than one "dead" deer has gotten up and run off when bowhunters trail too soon after the shot. Besides, if your buck is dead, he won't be any more dead when you finally walk up on him an hour or so later.

ON THE TRAIL

Tip #10: Pro shops are asked to help blood-trail deer every season, and Allen Miraglia of Scrubby Buck Archery in upstate New York is no exception. "All too often bowhunters want to get a gang of friends and go right after the deer," says Miraglia. "My best advice is to track your buck slowly, and to track him alone. This will keep you in control of the situation, giving you a better feel for what is really going on. For example, if your last blood splatter is on a faint deer run, chances are the next blood sign is just ahead on that same deer run. Just take your time and keep looking. Too many people tend to race ahead of each other hoping to find the next bit of sign, which, of course, can obliterate the trail, or worse, push the deer into no man's land if it is still alive."

Tip #11: Study blood drops and droplets carefully, as they can indicate the deer's exit trail. Generally, the splatters of blood are like fingers pointing out the direction of travel. Splatters that circle a blood drop, however, indicate the deer was standing still, maybe checking his back trail. Generally, bubbly blood is a lung hit, bright red blood is a muscle hit, and dark red blood is a liver, paunch, or even a heart hit.

Tip #12: Don't rely on the blood color to be your only clue to shot placement. If your arrow obviously went low and hit the brisket, you will find tallow on the arrow shaft. If it penetrated the body cavity, there will also be copious amounts of bright red blood. If your shot went wide and hit the paunch, the arrow will smell like feces. The amount of red blood from a muscle hit, although encouraging at first, will generally peter out within 200 yards if not actively pursued.

Tip #13: A double-lung-hit buck should travel far less than 200 yards before expiring. Any farther and he was probably not hit in both lungs.

Tip #14: Blood is not the only sign you should pay attention to when trailing a wounded deer. If

Blood-trailing is at best a one- or two-man job, but retrieving the deer sometimes requires all the help you can muster.

Examine the arrow shaft closely for evidence of a hit, including blood, hair, and bits of tissue. The shaft will smell like feces if the arrow entered the abdomen.

you get down on your hands and knees, you can often view the hoof prints of an escaping deer. This can be an important asset in the absence of blood. Look, too, for scuffmarks on the ground, broken twigs, flattened weeds, and turned-over leaves.

Tip #15: As you move about, do not disturb the blood trail, even if you are tracking on snow. You may have to reexamine the trail later. More than one buck has turned around 180 degrees and backtracked his own trail for several yards before continuing on in a different direction.

Tip #16: If you must seek help, remember that any more than three is a crowd. Do not talk, but rather use flashlights and hand signals to communicate. Don't give up the trail unless you are physically unable to continue. Get on your hands and knees if need be and continue to look for important clues.

TIMING IS EVERYTHING

Tip #17: If you believe the animal is mortally wounded but still alive, wait eight to ten hours before resuming.

Tip #18: If you believe the deer is hit in the paunch, wait at least twelve hours. Eighteen hours is even better. The blood can be extensive at first, but then it might diminish to just specks. If you watch the deer bed down, do not leave but keep a safe distance. Paunch-shot deer are known to get up after five or six hours and wander off for several hundred yards before lying down again.

Tip #19: If you believe the deer is hit in the liver, back off and wait four to six hours, with eight hours even better. The number one reason lethally shot deer are lost is that they are pushed off their deathbeds.

Tip #20: If you believe the deer has a serious but potentially non-lethal hit, such as a hit in the ham or a broken leg, then go right after the deer as soon as possible and do not stop until you catch up to him. Run him down "Indian-style" to keep the wound open.

Sometimes you have no choice but to wait overnight before resuming your search. It can be a sleepless night, however.

LOSE THE TRAIL?

Keep in mind that even a lethally shot animal may leave a sparse blood trail, and it can travel hundreds of yards before expiring. Here's what to do when the going gets tough.

Tip #21: Glance back on your trail markers to determine the line of travel and then proceed on your hands and knees in that direction. Closely examine

Ribbon trails can help you determine direction of travel, giving you an important clue should the blood inexplicably peter out.

There is always a risk coyotes will find your buck before you do, especially if you must abandon the trail at dark.

the "other" side of logs and blow-downs for blood. This is where you will often find blood if a wounded deer jumps these obstacles. Keep in mind that wounded deer rarely travel in a straight line, but will often circle around instead.

Tip #22: If a wounded deer enters a stream, look for water droplets on logs and rocks to indicate probable direction of travel. Wounded deer will also climb steep creek banks to elude pursuers.

Tip #23: Use your nose! I have located more than one dead buck by following the smell of musk in the air.

Tip #24: Use other animals. Crows, jays, and squirrels are often attracted to a deer carcass. I once located a dead buck by watching another buck stare intently into a brush pile. What was he looking at? My buck had crawled inside that brush pile and died.

Tip #25: Finally, a pool of blood generally indicates a resting area. If the blood trail stops there, then the buck may have turned at right angles or even 180 degrees to the trail and continued on, as deer will often change direction to avoid crossing open fields and busy highways or to take better advantage of available cover. He could also be dead nearby.

Lessons Learned 17

A whitetail buck is not an easy critter to tag with a bow and arrow.
Once he reaches maturity, he has
a bag of tricks like no other animal in the
forest. He can detect our presence with
superior senses and hightail it to parts
unknown, or he can hunker down and
hide in plain sight as we trudge by. And
if that is not enough to leave us talking to
ourselves, he can just as easily sneak past
us as we maneuver through his bailiwick
looking the wrong way!

A big buck is indeed the master of
his domain, but he is not unkillable. In
fact, the more we hunt him the more
likely we are to thwart his defenses and
have a close encounter. Oh, we might get
lucky once in a while and catch a big
buck flatfooted, but the real secret to consistently getting the drop on a whitetail
buck is to learn from our mistakes afield.

Indeed, over the years I have made
plenty of errors. They used to leave me
frustrated and disillusioned, but now I
treat them as blessings in disguise. That's
because each blunder has highlighted a
glaring weakness in my approach to
hunting deer, and over time, my efforts
to overcome these inadequacies have not
only made me a better woodsman but a

*Success breeds confidence, but often that
success comes after learning from our
mistakes afield.*

better deer hunter as well. Here are seven bucks I have missed still-hunting with the bow and arrow and the lessons I have learned from each.

OPENING DAY BUCK

I had him. It was that simple. It was the first day of the bow season, and I was still-hunting through an abandoned apple orchard when I caught some movement on the hillside above me. It was a buck, a decent eight-pointer, feeding on the fallen mast as he slowly worked his way through the orchard and towards the hay field below, where several does were feeding.

I nocked an arrow when he disappeared behind some weeds and then waited patiently for him to reappear. A few seconds later the whitetail stepped out into the clear only 12 or 14 yards in front of me, giving me an easy broadside shot. I quickly picked a spot low and behind his left shoulder and instinctively raised my recurve to shooting position. But at the last moment, I decided not to come to full draw. It was too early in the season to bushwhack a buck, I reasoned, especially when I knew the farm held several bigger deer, including a couple that would easily qualify for the record book.

I let the buck walk that evening. Much to my astonishment, I never saw him again. Nor did I see any of the real trophy deer I knew inhabited the farm.

Television personality Ray Eye nailed this buck from ground zero, and he did it on film.

I never did figure out where they went and never filled my home state bow tag that season. I was just too picky for my own good.

There is a lesson here: never pass up a buck the first day that you would be more than happy to tag on the last day of the hunt. Since then, I've bagged several bucks on opening day, including a fat eight-pointer I arrowed twenty minutes into the season. As the old saying goes, one in the hand is worth two in the bush!

CAUGHT FLATFOOTED

Here's another blooper. It was the peak of the rut, and the big, mature bucks were moving all day long. I had seen enough deer sign during the previous week to know that it was only a matter of time before a monster buck would step into view.

I was still-hunting in western Iowa with my bow this particular November morning when I happened to look down to see that I had waded through a thicket of pricker bushes. I was covered with the sticky little devils from my waist to my feet!

I immediately began pulling them off me, cursing myself for not being more attentive. I doubt more than a minute passed when for some reason I looked up to see a 250-plus-pound, yellow-tined ten-pointer staring at me from no more than 30 yards away! He had me pegged, and there was nothing I could do about it.

He didn't move a muscle, but when I tried to finesse an arrow onto the string—after what seemed like an eternity—the 140-class buck whirled, snorted once, and was suddenly gone from my life forever. I was sick to my stomach.

The lesson here is simple: still-hunting with archery tackle demands total concentration. Fortunately, I redeemed myself two days later by arrowing a mature buck while still-hunting along a scrape line. It pays to stay ever alert during the rut.

A buck can surprise you by showing up when and where you least expect him. Stay alert!

Don't ignore that inner voice that tells you something is not quite right. It could be a buck staring right at you.

HERE'S LOOKING AT YOU

One October morning I was still-hunting upwind with my bow through an abandoned farm field. The knee-high goldenrod and assorted weeds could not conceal a deer, I reasoned, and therefore I paid closer attention to the stand of oaks that bordered the old field. Buck sign was everywhere there, and by the heart-shaped tracks on the entry and exit trails, I could tell there had been plenty of deer feeding on the fallen mast in recent days.

Nonetheless, something fuzzy kept drawing my eyes out into the open field, but I paid it no heed. The feeling persisted, however, until I raised my binoculars and focused on that funny-looking object.

It was a buck's rack! He and a couple of does were bedded in the goldenrod some 50 or so yards away watching my every move. The deer soon sensed I had them spotted and were gone in a flash.

I learned many lessons from that encounter, including to always check out something that seems peculiar or out of place. A rutting buck will bed with a hot doe almost anywhere, and a buck facing danger will often remain bedded until the threat passes.

Since then, I have arrowed a couple of nice bucks in their beds—and passed on several smaller ones—by simply still-hunting crosswind and looking near the ground for those telltale horns.

RAINY-DAY WOMAN

I couldn't wait to get back into the woods. The rut was about to break wide open near my home in upstate New York and I had just the spot to go to, but when the weekend finally rolled around, bad weather dominated the scene. High winds coupled with occasional heavy rains kept most bowhunters at home near the fire.

Nonetheless, when dawn broke Saturday morning, I was pussyfooting along the edge of an overgrown field looking for deer and trying to stay out of the wind and rain. This particular abandoned farm was known to harbor some prodigious bucks, and I was sure that with the rut now in full swing I had a chance of at least seeing one of the wide-racked beauties.

I was not to be denied, for almost immediately a white flicker caught my attention. A doe, with her flag held at half-mast, was zigzagging across the goldenrod field, eventually passing within 25 yards or so of my kneeling position. And right behind her was a 130-class eight-pointer, weighing in at over 200 pounds on the hoof.

I remained kneeling, but when the buck trotted by, I figured he was a little over 25 yards away. Since he was oblivious to my presence, I decided to pass on the open shot and instead duck-walk along the edge of the field in an effort

to stay even with the buck. Surely, he would eventually swing closer to the edge of the woods, giving me an easier shot.

Well, it didn't work out that way. He didn't swing in closer to me but rather looped further out into the field. And then he sped up so I couldn't even stay even with him. I was suddenly left with only one option and that was to take a longer shot at a rapidly disappearing animal.

The buck stopped momentarily to look for the doe, and when he did I put my 40-yard pin on his chest and released a plastic-vaned aluminum shaft. I can still hear the "pift-pift-pift" of the arrow striking the raindrops as it sped towards the deer. By the time the broadhead arrived at the scene, however, the buck had switched ends, jumped 10 yards back, and was now looking in my direction as the arrow sailed harmlessly out into the goldenrod field. When the broadhead hit the dirt, the buck snorted and then bolted for the far side of the field.

Don't wait for a better shot. If you can kill him, do so right then and there!

Think twice before taking a shot in the rain. A heavy shower can wash away even a good blood trail in minutes.

I never saw him again, but that encounter left an indelible impression. Today, I take the first killing shot offered and never wait for a better one. And as far as hunting during a thunderstorm, I'll wait for the rain to stop before I step afield. I could have just as easily had a bad hit on that buck and then lost the blood trail in the heavy downpour.

SNEAK ATTACK

A buck can make a sudden appearance any time you are after him. In so doing, he might offer you a killing shot. But one year I had a buck walk right up behind me and startle me so badly I missed an easy opportunity. Here's what happened.

I was still-hunting along the base of a hardwood ridge littered with thousands and thousands of fat acorns. The deer were concentrated there, feeding on the bumper crop of mast with wild abandon. I was sure I was going to have some action that morning. And I did.

Keeping the wind in my face, I worked my way slowly up the hill, stopping every so often to survey the terrain before me. I hadn't gone 100 yards when something told me to turn around and look back down the hill. There, just 20 yards distant, was a buck working his way towards me, completely oblivious to my presence.

I dropped to one knee and nocked an arrow in one fluid motion, confident I was going to get a shot. By the time the buck caught up to me, however, I was shaking like a leaf in a windstorm. For some reason, all I could focus on was his shoulder blade. When the buck was broadside at 15 yards, I brought my 50-pound recurve to full draw and released a feathered shaft at his chest.

Much to my horror, the broadhead struck the buck—guess where?—on the shoulder blade and then fell out! The buck whirled and bounded away none the worse for the encounter. My ego, on the other hand, was bleeding profusely that day, leaving a gash that took months to heal.

Today, I pick a spot to shoot at *before* I come to full draw and then concentrate on that spot until after I release my arrow. This seems to eliminate those

errant shafts that hit where I am looking and not where I am aiming. I also
now shoot a modern cut-on-impact
broadhead with a tip that does not
curl over on impact.

THE MAPLE TREE BUCK

Several years ago a co-worker asked
me to take him bowhunting. He had
all the equipment and could shoot
decently enough; he just didn't have a
place to hunt. I showed him several
ambush sites on one of "my" farms,
and after much discussion, he elected
to hide near a blow-down just off a
heavily traveled trail. The deer were
feeding in a nearby field, and come
first light, we expected to waylay a
buck or two as they worked their way
towards the thick stuff to bed down
several hundred yards away. Since
Frank was not woods-wise, I thought
it best I still-hunt on a nearby ridge in
case he ran into trouble.

Well, the plan almost worked.
Soon after first light, I heard a commotion over in Frank's direction. He had
apparently missed a shot at a buck,
and the spooked animal was hightailing it in my direction. As luck would

*Pick a spot to shoot at before you come to
full draw. Otherwise, you may very well hit
what you are looking at, or worse, miss
altogether.*

have it, the buck practically walked right into my lap, offering me an easy
broadside shot.

The second the buck stepped into an opening, I came to full draw and
released. My arrow seemed true and struck with a resounding whack. I
thought I had scored a good hit, for the buck immediately kicked his heels up
and sprang back down the hill past Frank, who was now screaming, "You hit
him! You hit him!"

I rushed down to where Frank was standing and listened to him as he
related his version of the course of events. Then we went looking for my deer.
He showed me where the buck passed, but to our astonishment, there was no
blood. In fact, after several hours, we could not find any evidence of a hit.

Unless you find evidence to the contrary, always assume you hit the deer. If there is no blood in the immediate vicinity, look around for the buck's escape route, as evidenced by broken saplings and scuffed-up leaves. He may not start bleeding for 20, 30, or more yards.

I then went back up on the ridge, but it took me over an hour to pinpoint the exact scene of the shooting. And when I did, I found my arrow lodged in a four-inch maple tree halfway between the spot I was kneeling and the buck's splayed tracks. I had missed the buck clean!

I do things differently today. I still assume I hit every deer I shoot at until I find evidence to the contrary. However, I now mark the exact shooting location with orange flagging tape before I begin my search for blood and hair. And no matter what I find, I always proceed forward methodically from the shooting scene without cutting corners or rushing ahead 50 or more yards. It doesn't pay to take shortcuts when it comes to blood-trailing a whitetail buck.

PRAIRIE WHITETAIL

Dawn was still a half-hour away when I caught a trio of bucks working their way across the prairie a mile in the distance. I could plainly see that one of the bucks had a record-book rack, so I kept tabs on them until they bedded down along a fence line.

I marked the location in my mind then circled around to get the wind and the rising sun in my favor. A half-hour later I was standing in the thigh-high weeds looking for those bucks.

Suddenly, one of the smaller bucks stood up and walked over to a nearby drainage ditch to bed down again. I then glassed the grass in front of me, spotting the rack of the better buck bedded down about 30 yards away. It was amazing how well his antlers blended in with the dead grass. I wanted to shoot him in his bed, but I could not determine if his body was to the left or right of his rack, a common problem when you catch bucks in their beds. I figured I had plenty of time to make up my mind, so I knelt down to ponder my predicament. I knew the buck was not going anywhere soon.

Then providence took over because for some reason the buck chose that moment to stand up and stretch. He looked over in my direction but could not see me because he was looking directly into the rising sun.

I slowly came to full draw and put my 30-yard pin behind the buck's elbow without alerting him.

Do not change your mind once you determine the shooting distance. Invariably, you will miss by shooting over the buck's back.

He just stood there looking around like he was at a church social. Then doubt filled my mind. Was he 30 yards away, or was it closer to 35 or even 40 yards? At the last moment I raised my pin above the deer's back, and you guessed it, sent my broadhead sailing harmlessly over the buck's spine! I later paced off the distance from my orange marker (I was learning already) to the crushed vegetation in the buck's bed—30 yards on the nose.

Today I know better than to raise my pin. Once I estimate the yardage, I do not change my mind. I simply trust my instincts and shoot. I also practice estimating distances from both sitting and kneeling positions. That kind of practice helps, but it is not good enough. I have learned to also practice yardage estimation while looking over uneven terrain as well as open fields. Indeed, animals sometimes appear smaller standing out in a hay field than they do in thick cover. This phenomenon can fool you into believing the critter is farther away than he actually is, which, of course, can lead to a miss.

As you can see, I've made quite a few blunders in my day that have cost me some nice deer. I have also, however, learned some valuable lessons from my mistakes in the field. These lessons have helped me tag plenty of other nice deer.

What about you?

Thirty Hours with a Boone & Crockett Buck

18

I almost choked on my grunt tube. I was slowly still-hunting across a grassy ridge about an hour and a half before sunset when suddenly in the middle of a forty-acre cut cornfield stood a buck with a rack so striking it was clearly visible one-half mile away. I nervously yanked a variable grunt tube from inside my shirt and began to blow a series of notes I hoped would get the buck's attention. Unfortunately, the distance between us was too great.

The buck continued across the field in a casual manner and then entered the woodlot on the far side where I watched with amazement as he viciously attacked a sapling with his antlers before disappearing into the shadowy underbrush. I quickly crossed the field and entered the woodlot, but by the time I got there, the buck had long vanished.

I knew the buck would probably make the Big Book, but I had to get a better look at his rack before I could be certain. I returned to that grassy knoll the next evening and glassed until nearly dark, but the buck was nowhere to be seen. As legal shooting light waned, I turned to still-hunt my way back to the 4×4 when my eye caught something in

For a buck to grow a world-class set of antlers, he must survive his first year in the wild. Adverse weather conditions, malnutrition, predators, and accidents can account for a healthy share of button bucks. In some regions, coyotes alone can kill over half the crop in one summer.

the alders 65 yards away. I quickly raised my binoculars and saw "my" buck watching me with interest from the safety of the brush line.

He had caught me flatfooted, but before he hightailed it to parts unknown, I had time to take some mental measurements: He was a mainframe ten-pointer with 6-inch brow tines, 15-inch G-2s, 12-inch G-3s and 6-inch G-4s. The main beams curled up at the tips, making it difficult for me to determine if there were a set of G-5s in place, but they were heavy all the way to the tips and appeared to be at least 26 or 27 inches in length. Two sticker points on the right beam, although deductions, added character to the rack.

The inside spread was 25 or 26 inches, giving the buck that extra-wide boxlike look. I later tried to add the gross total in my head and arrived at 190-plus inches. I haven't seen a lot of bucks that big, either mounted or in the flesh, but I have held the number two buck from New York in my hands, the Reuben Haseley buck. It tallies 191. This Iowa buck was easily in the same class.

As soon as the buck realized I had him spotted, he whirled and disappeared into the brush. I was somewhat dejected, but I also realized few bowhunters are lucky enough to see a "Booner" in the wild. And I saw this bruiser two times in as many days! What more could a serious bowhunter ask for? Well, I didn't know it then, but the following week I would spend thirty hours with that buck—thirty hours that would leave me laughing, crying, hopeful, astonished, mesmerized, and finally just plain sick to my stomach. Here's what happened.

I believed my chances of seeing the monster buck again were quite good, seeing as I had access to over 12,000 acres of prime Iowa farmland. I cancelled all my other hunting plans and started a systematic search for that Iowa buck.

At first light a week later, I got that sighting. I was still-hunting the edge of that grassy knoll when I happened to catch my Booner standing next to a bedded a doe in the middle of that big cornfield. He had apparently been chasing her all night long, and she was plum tired. He nudged her to get her up, which she did, and then he approached her from behind. She began to flick her tail back and forth like a spawning hen steelhead, which really excited the old boy.

I nocked a razor-tipped shaft with shaking hands before nervously watching the spectacle unfold. The buck cocked his neck back and curled his lip, the classic flehmen response. Approaching her cautiously, he licked her genitals and then slowly put his front legs on her back, but she wasn't ready yet. She took one step forward, he slid off, and then she looked back at him. She repeated this coy maneuver a couple of times before finally letting the wide-racked buck mate. He passed his genes on several times, all the while pushing the doe in my direction.

Suddenly, a dinky yearling buck appeared out of nowhere and tried to get in on the action. The big buck pushed him away, but he was taking no chances and herded the doe away from me and across the corn lot into a small copse of trees and brush on the far side of the field. There he defended his right to the doe several times before bedding down next to her. I could easily see his rack glistening like a dance hall chandelier in the day's first light.

That's when I first got sick to my stomach. You see, that small copse of trees and brush was on a farm I had not yet secured permission to bowhunt. I had talked to one of the farmer's tenants who told me Mr. Smith only owned the cornfields, and since the corn was cut, I never bothered to pursue the matter further. Big mistake!

I watched the buck and doe until 9:30 that morning. He wasn't going to leave her soon, so I decided to go to him. But first, I had to track down that farmer. I started with the tenant, who very kindly telephoned the farmer, but the farmer's wife was unwilling to let me hunt the farm without first talking to her husband. I asked her where he was, and she said he was harvesting corn. I asked where, and she said about 20 miles away. I asked for directions,

Would it surprise you to learn that a three-and-a-half-year-old buck can sport a Boone & Crockett rack?

Biologists tell us a buck grows his best set of antlers between 4.5 and 6.5 years of age. But not all mature bucks grow big racks at this age. Genetics plays an important role.

which were complicated. You know, take a right at the old tree hit by lightning, then a left by the dried-up farm pond. Stay on that dirt road until you come to your second dirt road on the left. . . . I wrote it all down and set out in search of the farmer. How long would that buck and doe stay bedded? Not all day, I surmised, so I had to rush.

I finally found Mr. Smith atop a huge harvester. I waved to him when he came to the end of the field, and he motioned me up into the cab. Now keep in mind that I am driving a truck with out-of-state plates, I am dressed in full camo, including face paint, and I have never talked with this farmer before. He had no idea who I was or what I wanted. But after 30 minutes of small talk, he signed my business card, which allowed me to hunt his farm. As I crawled out of the cab—sweaty armpits and all—he told me there was a big buck on the farm. He had seen the tracks but didn't know how big the rack was. I wanted to tell him how big, but declined. I was afraid he'd change his mind.

It was now 11:30 A.M. After finding my way back to the farm, I grabbed my bow and headed for the copse of trees and brush. I was filled with anticipation until I happened to look down at my arrow rest. Somewhere along the route I had bent the rest! I almost passed out. Fortunately, I shoot fingers, and bringing the rest back to specs only took a few minutes. After a few bull's-eyes on some nearby hay bales, I was back in business.

Finally, after what seemed like a never-ending nightmare, I started still-hunting along the edge of the trees. Suddenly, the dinky buck jumped up in front of me and ran off. I was flabbergasted because he was bedded only 15 yards away, and I hadn't seen him. What if he had been "my" buck? I asked myself. I slowed down and kept my eyes open.

Five minutes later, my Booner nonchalantly stepped out of the copse in front of me 80 yards distant, minus the doe. He looked over at me, looked away, and then did a double take at my quivering mass of jelly. The buck snorted and hightailed it over the ridge. I gave chase, of course, and watched as he ran over a mile in a wide circle through cornfields and brush lots only to disappear near the same grassy knoll I was standing on earlier in the morning.

Exhausted, I returned to my 4×4 and fell asleep. It had already been a long day. As it turned out, I would need that extra shut-eye because my encounter with this Iowa buck was only half over.

I woke up an hour later with a plan for the evening hunt. I would slowly still-hunt the edge of the cornfield and grassy knoll. With any luck, I might just catch that buck patrolling the brush line for an amorous doe. And as luck would have it, that's just what happened!

About sunset, a small eight-pointer sauntered past me at 25 yards. He took me by surprise because he had come from behind me. When I back-tracked him with my eyes, I saw my Booner chasing a doe around, 300 yards

To grow old in some parts of the country, bucks need a sanctuary, such as posted property or property that is impenetrable by most people.

A nutritious winter food source is paramount for survival in snow country.

off to my right. I quickly closed the distance and pulled an arrow from my quiver.

To my chagrin, the doe turned around and ran along the edge of the grassy knoll on the same trail as the eight-pointer, taking the Booner with her. If I had stood still for just five minutes, that doe would have led that buck past me at 25 yards. I was getting sick again.

By this time, there was a trio of does and a couple of small bucks gathered just off the grassy knoll feeding in an alfalfa lot. I worked my way to the edge of that field and glassed. The Booner was busy checking out the does and oblivious to my intentions. I couldn't believe my good fortune.

I pulled out my fawn bleat and blew a few quiet notes. The doe nearest the buck picked her head up and looked over in my direction. I blew another fawn bleat and then a deep grunt from my variable grunt tube. She was definitely interested. When she dropped her head, I nocked an arrow and blew another note with my fawn call. She jerked her head up and started walking in my direction with the Booner in tow.

I dropped to one knee and readied myself for the shot. At 40 yards, she turned broadside and started to feed, but the buck was shielded by the doe and still walking towards me. I didn't have the right angle. Suddenly, she caught my wind, whirled, and ran out of the field along a drainage ditch, taking the buck with her.

I yanked out my grunt tube, but it was to no avail. She was not interested, and the buck could care less. I had done my best, and the deer had won. Exhausted, I snuck back to my truck to reflect on the day's events. Nothing could top my experiences that day. Nothing except perhaps what happened the very next morning near that very same cornfield. I would get one more chance to arrow that giant Iowa whitetail!

Reasoning the buck would still be in the vicinity of the hot does, I arrived back on the grassy knoll under starlight to wait for legal shooting hours. I caught a flash of white at pink light and soon spotted the Booner chasing a doe around in a CRP field adjacent to the big cornfield.

He was very alert that morning, much more so than the previous day. I watched through my binoculars as he played the game of love with that doe, chasing her up a hill and then out into the field. But he knew something wasn't quite right. Maybe he saw me or heard me moving through the frost-covered goldenrod. Whatever it was, he decided to exit the scene.

A loud guttural grunt caught his attention, however. He stared back in my direction for a full 15 minutes, frozen in position like a deer on a Christmas card. It took a soft fawn bleat to convince him the coast was clear. He flicked his tail and started walking up a hedgerow in my direction.

Ask your local taxidermist and he will tell you the biggest bucks seem to come from the same county, often the same hillside, year after year.

Although luck certainly plays a role in some cases, dedicated deer hunters have the edge when it comes to tagging monster bucks.

What happened next I do not know for sure. I knelt down in the tall grass near the hedgerow and waited for him to step into view, but the buck never showed. I finally put my arrow back in the quiver and looked around for him, but he had walked out of my life forever. Indeed, I spent the next two weeks looking for that buck, but I never saw hide or hair of him again.

I think back about those thirty hours now and feel privileged to have played hide-and-seek with such a smart animal. And not out of a treestand, mind you. No, we shared the same topography, the same ground cover, and the same wind. I watched him strut his stuff out in the open as well as in the thick stuff. And I watched him pass on his genes.

Indeed, those thirty hours were the time of my life with the buck of a lifetime!

PART IV
Still-Hunting with Firearms

How to Wear Blaze Orange Effectively

19

Much to the dismay of the animal rights crowd, hunting is a safe sport. It is safer than swimming, fishing, boating, and canoeing, and in terms of trips to the emergency room, football, basketball, hockey, and a host other contact sports prove to be far more dangerous than a lone woodsman still-hunting along a hickory ridge in search of a wide-racked buck.

Hunter Education has certainly played a major role in making hunting a safe pursuit. And so has blaze orange. Indeed, this unnatural color helps prevent hunters being mistaken for game as well as keeping them out of the line of fire. And if a hunter is lost or becomes ill when afield, an orange cap or vest can help search and rescue workers quickly locate him from the ground or from the air.

There are rules governing the use of blaze orange, and they can vary from province to province, state to state, and sometimes from one county to the next. Some states and provinces strongly recommend

Deer hunting is a relatively safe sport due in part to hunter education and the widespread use of fluorescent hunter or blaze orange.

Choose soft fabrics with dull finishes like cotton or twill. Stay away from canvas outerwear and plastic vests; they make too much noise!

its usage, whereas other states and provinces mandate that hunters wear so many square inches on certain parts of their body, anything from a cap to several hundred square inches on their head, chest, back, and shoulders. Whatever the rules, make sure you check local regulations before stepping afield—and then abide by them.

Unbelievably, there are deer hunters out there who still refuse to wear blaze orange, whether it is mandated by law or not. Some are poachers and trespassers who want to do their dirty work without being seen. Others are more concerned with being picked off by a whitetail and feel their chances of tagging a good buck are diminished if they comply with any local blaze orange regulations.

Biologists are still not sure how deer perceive color, especially blaze orange, but one thing is for certain. There is plenty of anecdotal evidence to suggest a deer will see a hunter dressed head-to-toe in fluorescent orange before it will see a hunter dressed from head-to-toe in modern camouflage. And you can bet grandpa's old Winchester on that!

How then can you remain safe, comply with the law, and still get close to a white-tailed deer? It is easier than you think, and in fact, in most cases it is just common sense. Take outerwear for example. The first step towards using blaze orange more effectively is to pick a fabric that is not as shiny as vinyl or some of the cheap plastics. If you shop around, you will come across several fabrics with a dull finish, like cotton knit or brushed twill. Cabela's, Bass Pro Shops, and other major outdoor outlets have plenty of blaze or hunter orange garments to choose from that not only comply with local laws, but are quiet, too. Indeed, nothing destroys the serenity of a morning's still-hunt faster than a branch slapping up against a cold plastic hunting vest.

There is another class of outerwear that can help you hide from the prying eyes of a whitetail deer and still keep you safe. These garments are crinkle cut during the manufacturing process to give you a leafy or 3-D appearance. What is so special about 3-D? Any large block of fabric, no matter what color it is, reflects a lot of light back to the animal. It is this reflected light that gives that block of fabric the perception of form, making a human hunter easily recognizable in the woods.

A good camouflage design can go a long way towards breaking up that human outline, but 3-D outerwear takes it to a higher plane. A blaze-orange jacket, for example, cut to 3-D no longer has a flat surface to reflect a lot of light. Instead, the 3-D cut of the jacket breaks up the block of fabric by giving it texture and more natural shading. Indeed, 3-D clothing reflects less light, making the wearer less likely to be seen by a wary whitetail buck.

Does your hunting garment have to be solid blaze orange? In some locales the answer is yes, but where legal, blaze-orange camouflage, with its black

A soft blaze-orange cap and vest coupled with 3-D camouflaged outwear can keep you safe, legal, and go a long way towards breaking up your human outline.

Where legal, avoid wearing hunter orange on your extremities, as the color accentuates movement.

blotches and squiggles printed on top of a solid blaze-orange background, can go a long way towards breaking up your human outline, too. Be aware, however, that those blotches and squiggles take away from the total amount of blaze orange in the garment. And in those states and provinces where you are required to wear so many square inches of blaze orange, you may have to increase the size or number of garments to fully comply with the law. Nonetheless, blaze-orange camouflage can indeed be very effective and should be your first choice of blaze-orange garment. But what if your state does not allow an orange camouflage pattern and you must instead wear a great deal of solid blaze orange on your upper torso?

Where legal, try to refrain from wearing blaze orange on your head, arms, hands, and legs whenever possible. Deer are keen on picking out objects that move, and few colors accentuate movement as much as blaze orange, in part because this color contrasts sharply with any natural background.

Try this exercise, a favorite of mine, and I think you will see what I mean. Have a friend position himself 75 yards away—the average distance most deer are taken with a shotgun—and wave at you with a camouflaged glove on one hand a florescent orange glove on the other. Which hand grabs your attention? Imagine how easy it would be for a buck to pick you off if you were also wearing an orange hat, pants, and a full-sleeve jacket!

Nonetheless, you must still break up the human blob created by that solid block of blaze orange worn on your chest, back, and shoulders as much as possible. A blaze-orange vest, for example, worn over a camo jacket will begin to do the job nicely, especially if that jacket is cut to 3-D.

You can take this approach one step further by mixing and matching various camouflage patterns. You do not need to be a slave to fashion, however. In fact, a hat, jacket, shirt, and pants in different name brands, combined with a solid or 3-D blaze-orange vest, can be very effective at breaking up the human outline.

The rule of thumb is to match the clothing below your waist to what is on the ground, and match what is above your waist to the predominant color scheme above the ground. For example, when the ground is littered with dead leaves, as it so often is here in the east during the regular firearms season, I prefer to wear pants in a brown camouflage pattern. If I am going to be in the hardwoods, then my hat and jacket will be a gray camouflage pattern. If I am going to be prowling around a swamp where evergreens grow, then a dark camo jacket with some green in it will more than suffice.

Later in the season when fresh snow covers the ground and the snow is still falling, I will wear a blaze-orange vest over a one-piece snow-camo outfit. But if the snow has stopped falling and winds have knocked the snow off the tops of branches and weeds, then I will wear snow-camo bottoms and a gray camo jacket and hat with a blaze-orange vest.

These are all killer combinations, but don't stop there. You also want to camouflage your face, neck, and ears as well as your hands and wrists. Your head and arms move more than any other body part, and with blaze or hunter orange on, you are more likely to attract a deer's attention. Besides, the closer you are to the ground the more likely your uncovered shiny skin will seem out of place to an alert buck—even if he doesn't catch you moving!

Finally, leave your bright stainless steel rifle home, or if you must hunt with it, be sure you apply camo tape to the barrel, receiver, scope, and scope mounts. Walking through the woods with a shiny gun is like waving a flashlight in the dark. The bucks are going to see it and vamoose before you are even remotely aware they were nearby.

Snow camo, when coupled with the required amount of blaze orange, can be deadly on whitetails. I would nix the orange snowshoes, however.

EYE TO EYE

It is now more important than ever to stick to thick cover when still-hunting in fluorescent orange, especially after leaf drop or when there is snow on the ground. And you do this by looking hard for the next piece of cover as you still-hunt through the deer woods. I may still-hunt more slowly along the inside of a hedgerow, stopping periodically next to a large diameter tree, a boulder, an old log, a stump, or a blow-down to help break up my human outline. I might also use topographical features such as old creek beds, irrigation ditches, ridgelines, and canyon rims to move along with just my head and shoulders visible above the forest floor. Indeed, keeping low to the ground and having something in front of you to help break up your human outline is often the key to success whether you have blaze orange on or not.

One year while practicing stop-and-go rattling I lured in a wide-racked western eight-point after dropping into some brush along a creek bed to grind some bone. Even though I was wearing the required amount of blaze orange, that buck still got to within spitting distance of me before spooking. He snorted and vamoosed when he saw me, but it was too late. My '06 caught up to him, dropping him in his tracks with one well-placed shot less than 100 yards distant.

BOWHUNTING THE GUN SEASON WITH BLAZE ORANGE

When the bowhunting bug bites, it often leaves us thirsty for more action. To get our adrenaline going, we soon forego hunting whitetails with a gun, opt-

Bowhunters who hunt during the regular firearm season must comply with gun-season rules governing the use of blaze orange. Orange rattling horns are optional.

ing instead to hunt them with archery tackle throughout the regular firearm season. And therein lies the rub. How can we dress in camouflage and bowhunt safely when there are thousands of gun hunters in the deer woods?

In most states, if you want to bowhunt deer during the open season, you must abide by gun-season rules, and that means you must wear so many square inches of blaze-orange clothing on certain parts of your body. Even in states were blaze orange is not mandatory, such as my home state of New York, wearing some blaze orange, even it is only a vest, is often a good idea, especially when walking to and from your hunting area. You do not want to be mistaken for a white-tailed deer trying to sneak past a concealed gun hunter.

Keep in mind that even in states with high compliance rates, there are always five to ten or more hunters per hundred that do not wear the required amount of blaze orange as prescribed by law. Their actions can pose a substantial safety risk to bowhunters who hunt deer during the regular firearm season. Why? Because if wearing blaze orange is mandatory, then there will always be some hunters who believe that if something moves and is not wearing blaze-orange clothing, then it must be a deer. This mindset can make a bowhunter in full camo quite vulnerable. Even if you are hunting private property, it behooves you to always display enough blaze orange to keep from being mistaken for a deer.

In addition, keep in mind that in many states it is illegal to shoot a gun or a bow after sunset during the regular season. This is true even though there is still plenty of light to shoot a bow accurately—and even though you could shoot a half-hour after sunset during the early bow season. Bowhunters who hunt deer during the firearm season must be very careful to obey this law and not shoot their bow

Even if fluorescent orange is not mandatory where you hunt, it is a good idea to put some on when dragging a buck back to camp, especially after sunset.

Muzzleloaders and bowhunters might opt for wearing orange during overlapping late-season hunts. They may mistakenly believe they are alone in the deer woods.

after the close of legal hunting hours. The deer they think they see could very well be one of those non-compliant hunters on his way home to have supper with his wife and kids.

NO SUCH THING AS TOO MUCH BLAZE ORANGE

Of course, there will also be times when you do want everybody to see you wearing blaze orange. You don't want to be mistaken for a deer, especially in dim light, when sneaking in and out of your hunting grounds. Even walking across an open field before first light can be a dangerous exercise, especially on opening day when anxious deer hunters are more apt to take senseless chances by shooting at deer in the dark.

You also want to wear hunter orange when you are trailing a wounded deer on your hands and knees, and even later on, when you're dragging your buck back to camp. Indeed, this is when you want your blaze-orange cap and gloves to accentuate your body movements. You want to be seen!

You might also want to consider wearing a hunter-orange vest during the regular bow season whenever you are sneaking in and out of your hunting grounds, especially if you're deer hunting on land open to the public. A poacher in his stand before or after legal shooting hours could easily mistake your gait for that of a feeding deer and take a shot at you in the dark. It has happened on at least one occasion, killing the bowhunter.

Wearing blaze orange is also an option for those safety-conscious deer hunters who want to wear some protective clothing during the late bow and muzzleloader seasons, especially when the two overlap. Hunters of both persuasions can be lulled into believing they are the only hunters in the woods, which can lead to taking chances they otherwise would not consider.

A strip of orange flagging tape or an orange vest can help you find a downed deer and get it out of the woods before darkness settles in. Check local laws governing transporting deer after shooting hours.

Finally, whenever I hunt the big woods, like the wilds of New Brunswick or the Adirondack Mountains in upstate New York, I generally pack a blaze-orange vest and a roll of blaze-orange surveyor's tape in my daypack in case I have to leave my tagged buck to get help with the dragging chores. These bucks are hard enough to shoot but thankfully easier to find with a ribbon trail and a buck's rack covered with a blaze-orange vest. This is where blaze orange really shines!

20 The Connection is Clear-Cut

Clear-cuts attract bucks like moths to an open flame. And for good reason! They provide food, cover, and the open spaces deer crave.

It always comes as a surprise. Sure, we can anticipate the occasion by careful planning, hours of practice, and intense concentration in the field. We can even dream of what to do when that special time arrives. Nonetheless, events can unfold quickly on a deer hunt, giving us precious little time to decide on a course of action. Often, that's when instinct takes over.

Such was the case for trophy hunter Carmen Cavaleri. He was hunting near a clear-cut in northwestern Montana a few years back when the opportunity of a lifetime suddenly presented itself.

"My guide spotted a world-class buck in this clear-cut the day before," explains Cavaleri, "so we decided to set up a treestand along a line of trees in the middle of the opening in hopes the buck would return. The next morning dawned cold, but I stayed aloft until around 10 o'clock. I decided to still-hunt along the periphery of the clear-cut then for a look-see and to warm up a little.

"I hadn't gone too far when I heard what sounded like a deer stamping its foot. I looked over to my left out in the clear-cut and saw a doe staring right at me. She immediately hightailed it into the brush, taking a huge buck with her in hot pursuit. A smaller buck, however, was left standing out in the open; he apparently had no idea what was going on. I quickly found him in my scoped Remington .270 and, with little hesitation, touched off a 150-grain Nosler Partition. The buck bolted for 50 yards, but another Federal Premium from my Mountain Rifle also found its mark, dropping the 7×6 at 125 yards.

"I couldn't believe how heavy he was! My guide and I both estimated his live weight to be about 305 pounds, a big buck in any part of the continent. Later, after the mandatory 60-day drying period, his massive rack taped out at 164 ⅝, making it my best buck to date."

Indeed, Cavaleri's buck was a wall-hanger. I was in camp when Jon Kayser's 4×4 pulled up to the bunkhouse with that buck in the back, and I can testify to the wide grin on Cavaleri's face, proving once again that clear-cuts are magnets for big bucks. What's the attraction? According to Wade Nolan, founder and producer of the Whitetail University Video series, there are two good reasons for this.

"First, whitetails are edge animals," says Nolan, "and as such, they tend to gravitate towards ecotones, which are places where different types of habitat join. Clear-cutting a mature forest creates a lot of edge, and if it occurs in a wilderness setting, it may be the only edge in town. Here is what usually happens.

"For the first two years in the life of a clear-cut, grasses grow freely because the sun can now actually shine on dirt. Then plants, like red osier, honeysuckle, greenbrier, white cedar, maple, and willow take over. They tend to grow from the ground to the 40-inch level, where whitetails spend most of their time eating. Now, this becomes important in November. That's when deer stop grazing on grasses and start feeding more on browse.

"Secondly, clear-cuts can also become core areas," adds Nolan, "a concept pioneered by Dr. Jim Byford at the University of Tennessee. A core area is a point of focus within the home range of a white-

Well-earned braggin' rights back at camp for Cavaleri!

Clear-cuts can become core areas for mature bucks where they spend most of their time feeding and bedding.

tail where that deer spends most of its time feeding and bedding. The notion of a bedding area remaining static day after day is not true. Research has shown that bedding locations change in concert with peaking food sources. In farm country, for example, bucks may bed near a clover field during the summer and then near a harvested corn lot as winter draws near.

"However, a wilderness clear-cut can become a long-term core area, especially during mid-winter, whenever it provides a primary food source (browse), a safe bedding area, and ample cover. It thus supplies everything a deer needs to survive in one location."

Keeping Nolan's comments in mind, here is how three leading whitetail outfitters get trophy bucks from wilderness clear-cuts.

SASKATCHEWAN

"Whitetails are attracted to clear-cuts faster than many people think," says Zane Pikowicz of Saskatchewan's Pierceland Outfitters. "In fact, they are often drawn first to the sound of a power saw. You see, when a wilderness area is first logged, deer will immediately begin feeding on the mosses suddenly made available to them because the trees are now lying on the ground. They will graze there later as various grasses take root and then browse in the months and years ahead as various woody plants take hold.

"Clear-cuts are in many ways like fields," adds Pikowicz. "Deer take advantage of terrain features and any available cover to enter a clear-cut, to cross from one side to the next, and to eventually exit the opening to get back into the bush. They have feeding routes inside and along the edges of the clear-cut runways circling just outside the clear-cut, and preferred travel routes connecting one clear-cut with another. They tend to use each according to the wind, available food, the rut, and hunting pressure.

"As you know, mature bucks are vulnerable during the rut, but they are not stupid. Before one will enter a big open clear-cut, he will likely check it first for danger. They also have a tendency to hang in the woods and follow the edges, trying to stay under cover as much as possible."

Scout a wilderness clear-cut like a farm field. Deer will use terrain features and available cover to move about undetected. Notice the shotgun, a weapon preferred by some who hunt their bucks in the thick stuff.

NEW BRUNSWICK

"A good deer hunter can spend a week in New Brunswick," adds retired outfitter Jerry Trecartin, "and only get one chance at a trophy buck. That buck, however, will probably be the biggest deer he has ever seen in the wild. You see, we do not have as many deer as our farm-country brethren, but what we lack in numbers, we more than make up for in size.

"Deer don't show themselves much here and that makes them even harder to hunt," says Trecartin. "Many people believe that's because they spend a lot of time watching their back trail for coyotes. In any event, rattling is not as effective here in part because of low deer densities and the fact that the most productive times to be afield are the last two weeks of the season—the peak of the rut."

The best places to locate New Brunswick bucks are undoubtedly in and around clear-cuts. The better cuts here are four or five years old with head-high cover and lots of shoots. "A buck could be 100 yards away in one of these clear-cuts," says Trecartin, "but you won't see him because of all the vegetation. Good binoculars and sometimes a spotting scope are a must as some of these clear-cuts are three or four miles across."

IDAHO

Jon Kayser has nearly twenty years of experience guiding for western whitetails in Idaho. Although as successful on the open prairie as he is in the big woods, his favorite whitetail producer has always been clear-cuts. Why? "Because you can always count on finding mature bucks working the cuts, especially during the peak of the rut," says Kayser. "I always figure Thanksgiving Day to be the best day to be afield for trophy deer.

"Nonetheless, when deer hunting wilderness clear-cuts, don't overlook adjacent terrain features for racked deer. These can be hot spots onto themselves, if you are willing to take the time and scout them out properly.

"Plateaus just above a clear-cut, for example, are always worth scouting," advises Kayser. "Bucks will often use these as staging areas, preferring to mill around here until darkness falls before descending to the cut to feed. These are also great locations for scrapes, scrape lines, rubs, and, of course, rub lines. Look for bucks to enter the plateau from nearby high ground, such as a knoll, ridge, or high peak.

Binoculars and spotting scopes can help you locate travel routes in those mile-long cuts from the opposite hillside.

Whitetail expert Jon Kayser likes to key in on staging areas above the clear-cut where bucks will mill around before descending to the cut to feed.

"Next, look for gentle slopes, spurs, and ravines to funnel deer to and from the cut. These are great travel lanes for the avid still-hunter. The presence of fresh rubs and large tracks should help to pinpoint the best trails. Finally, consider those connecting routes between adjacent clear-cuts as these can be especially productive once the rut kicks into high gear. Bucks will be moving between clear-cuts 24/7 in their seemingly never-ending search for a doe near estrus. Strips of timber and brush-lined creek beds are both worth a second look-see when the 'moon of madness' strikes."

CLASSIC STILL-HUNT

I knew the buck was in there, somewhere, and would likely appear soon after the storm abated. Jon and I had scouted the area earlier that morning and found plenty of tracks, including some large splayed specimens that sunk deep into the earth. Other tracks covered the corner of the old clear-cut, telling us there were plenty of does frequenting the area. With the rut near high gear, these girls were probably attracting several mature bucks to the cut, including at least one that was leaving those tracks and fresh 4-inch rubs along the perimeter.

We rattled a bit along one of the exit trails, with no luck. We then decided rather than linger any longer we would sneak back into the opening, being careful not to disturb the area any more than what we already had, and return later. As it turned out, we made the right decision because late that afternoon I had a run-in with that buck, a big thirteen-point typical that left my heart pumping like a racehorse at Churchill Downs.

As predicted, the storm blew itself out and the winds died down by mid-afternoon. Jon dropped me off a half-mile distant, and while he drove away to hunt a nearby burn, I began to slowly still-hunt just inside the wood line of that cut. An hour passed with no buck sightings. At one point, all was dead quiet; then I caught some movement 100 yards into the cut. It was a buck, and a real shooter, moving steadily across the opening en route to a copse of trees left behind by the bulldozer, a known doe bedding area.

Somehow that buck sensed I was there. Maybe he caught me in mid-stride or maybe he caught a stray wisp of human odor; whatever the case, he had me pinpointed. There was no time to check his tines with my binoculars, and there was certainly no time to crank up my scope. I would have to be satisfied with my initial judgment that this was a humdinger of a buck and take the 100-yard shot with my scope set at 1.5x.

Without wasting a second, I grabbed a 3-inch sapling for support

Bucks enter clear-cuts using terrain features and whatever other cover is available to remain undetected.

and shouldered my .30-06, resting it atop my clenched wrist before centering his chest in the crosshairs. At the shot, the buck turned and ran back towards the corner of the cut, tail out and looking unharmed. With the open hillside serving as a safe backstop, I pumped another round into the chamber, and before the spent casing hit the ground, I shot again. This time I thought I saw the buck flinch, but he was up to full speed now, kicking up loose soil with each leap and bound. I pumped another round and shot a third time just before he reached the wood line, but this one didn't stop him, either. When he turned to run an old logging road, I fired once more, but this time I pulled the shot, subconsciously fearing the bullet might strike that magnificent rack.

It was all over in seconds, and my initial reaction was not good. The first three shots felt like they were on the money, but the buck ran as if I had missed him clean with each round. I was sure Jon had heard my shots, and rather than face the music, I decided right then and there to

Despite my initial fears, I found the buck piled up a short distance away.

tell him a bold-faced lie about emptying my clip on a coyote. I knew he wouldn't believe me, but that was going to be my story, for a while anyway.

How could I have missed?, I asked myself as I ejected the empty clip and jacked my spare into the pump. Not wanting to waste any time, I gave chase. If I had only wounded the buck, and he got into the softwood timber, I would have a hard time finding his blood trail. With any luck, I would hear him crashing away through the underbrush, giving me at least a direction of travel to go by.

My worries were unfounded, however, for I soon found my buck piled up just inside the wood line with three hits, any one of which could have been the killer. I was relieved, to say the least. After tagging and field dressing the buck, I chuckled to myself. Now I wouldn't have to tell Jon about the coyote that got away!

Later, we put a generous tape on the rack. It grossed in the mid-170s, but lack of symmetry, a split G-2, and two abnormal points would keep him out of the Big Book—as if it really made that much of a difference. He was a heckuva buck, and I was glad to get him! ■

Study appropriate topographical maps before entering a clear-cut. It can save you a lot of time by helping you pinpoint terrain features bucks crave.

STILL-HUNTING STRATEGIES

My favorite technique for hunting clear-cuts has always been still-hunting. In fact, my two heaviest New Brunswick bucks were bagged while still-hunting, dressing out at 200 and 220 pounds, respectively.

The trick to still-hunting wilderness clear-cuts is careful scouting, and all reconnoitering should begin with a long look at a topographical map. First, key in on adjacent terrain features that attract mature bucks. Natural waterways such as beaver dams, lake and pond shorelines, and riverbeds are a good start. Next, look for gentle slopes leading in and out of walled canyons, nearby brushy draws, and, of course, steep ravines, especially if they connect one clear-cut with another. Then look for plateaus, high peaks, and saddles between those peaks that are within walking distance. Finally, be sure to check out any nearby manmade openings such as power lines, logging truck staging areas, and abandoned cart roads. All these features are magnets for rutting bucks.

As soon as possible, you want to check all these features for fresh deer sign, including tracks and fresh droppings, and fresh "buck works," including ravaged rubs, large scrapes, and my favorite, smoking hot scrape lines. Indeed, over the years I have had more close encounters with mature big-woods bucks by pussyfooting along the downwind edge of a fresh scrape line than any other big-woods deer hunting strategy.

To be honest, buck works can sometimes be difficult to find in any big-woods setting. However, I have discovered that if I superimpose aerial photography with topographical maps my chances of finding scrapes and scrape lines increase ten-fold. What do you look for? That's easy! As mentioned earlier, any opening in the forest canopy will attract rutting bucks, but long-grown-over clear-cuts and the logging roads that served them have proven to be the most productive.

Note that these are not your average clear-cuts but rather ones that are ten to fifteen or more years old. Hence the difficulty the average hunter has in locating the perimeter of the clear-cut and the need for aerial photography.

One year, after studying a block of topo maps and black and white aerial photographs, I located a funny white line on one of the photographs that did not match up with any structure on the topo map. I suspected the white line, which denoted an absence of tall forest, was in fact an old logging road. I investigated and found a crisscrossed network of abandoned logging roads that apparently serviced an age-old clear-cut. Best of all, several of the logging roads were littered with scrapes and scrape lines. It was as if I had stumbled upon the mother lode of all wilderness deer! I had to leave the next day, but a friend of mine hunted the old roads and nailed a majestic 150-class ten-pointer, the smaller of the two deer he caught freshening the buck works before 10 o'clock the next morning.

CALLING STRATEGIES

Clear-cuts serve an additional function during the rut. They allow rutting bucks to cover lots of ground in a short period of time in their seemingly endless search for an estrous doe. In fact, if you can simply keep your eyes on a cut and use the right vocalization at the right time, you might just get a crack at a real trophy.

Indeed, the peak of the rut offers more calling opportunities for the still-hunter, and hence more chances for

When deer densities are low, bucks will frantically seek out any hint of an estrous female, making fawn bleats and other vocalizations a hot strategy for the lone still-hunter.

Power lines, gas lines, and other rights-of-way also attract bucks in much the same manner as clear-cuts. This buck responded to my estrous doe bleats long enough for me to snap his picture.

success, than any other time of the year. Bucks are so frantic for love now that the sight, sound, or smell of an estrous female is often all it takes for them to throw caution to the wind—at least for a short period of time—and rush in to claim all breeding rights.

Let's say you spy a mature buck weaving in and out of cover some distance out in the cut, obviously seeking out estrous does. He takes a few steps, sniffs the air and then the ground while looking intently all around. What would be your vocalization of choice? A long and drawn out fawn bleat. Why? The key word is "mature." A young buck may pay little or no heed, but a mature buck may know from past experience that a fawn looking for its mother can often only mean one thing: the doe is nearby being bred by another buck. That plaintiff wail may be all it takes for him to circle downwind and sneak in for a look-see.

Now let's say you see a mature doe on the edge of the cut being hounded by a mature buck, both of which could disappear at any moment. She is obviously trying to elude him, probably because she is still a day or so away from ovulating. The buck instinctively knows this and tries to keep his distance without running her off. What vocalization might you try? A doe contact grunt. Her behavior tells you she would like to dump her suitor, and one way for her to do this is to get him interested in another doe, possibly one closer to estrus. She will respond to your call, with the old boy in tow, in an effort to lose the buck by crossing trails with a second (or even a third, hint!) female.

As you can see, clear-cuts are to wilderness bucks what cornfields are to farmland deer, and you can hunt them just like you would a farmer's crop field back home. Keep in mind the wisdom of Wade Nolan and the fact that some clear-

A week of still-hunting Montana clear-cuts.

cuts offer whitetails everything: food, cover, and a bedding area. If you do not see where bucks are entering a clear-cut, you may have to go take a second look at the interior. After all, Carmen Cavaleri did!

21 Stalking Bucks on Thunder Road

Do bucks like nasty weather? Sometimes!

I pulled the 4×4 onto a jeep trail and shut off the engine. Shooting light was only a half-hour away, but I sat in the cab wondering what to do. High gusting winds were rocking the truck back and forth, and the heavy rains that had been predicted were starting to fall. I turned my Sirius satellite radio to the Weather Channel, hoping for a reprieve, but it was not in the forecast. It was destined to be one miserable day afield.

No buck would be up and about in this kind of weather, I reasoned, so I poured a second cup of coffee and waited for the first hint of day. I started to drift off when it suddenly struck me like a bolt of lightning. Of course the deer wouldn't be up and about under these conditions. They would be, instead, holed up on the lee side of the hill, maybe in the planted pine plantation or just inside the thick edge of the swamp.

I grabbed my wool jacket and stepped out of the truck. There was no time to waste, so I hastily stuffed a sandwich and a bottle of water into the game bag and uncased my '06. Five minutes later I was 100 yards down the jeep trail teeming with excitement. I just knew I was going to get a crack at a nice buck. And soon!

Dawn was quickly approaching, so I quickened my pace, allowing the howling winds and occasional thunderclap to mask my forward progress. When I reached the meadow at the top of the hill I slowed down and turned due east, quartering into the wind. I followed an old hedgerow for several hundred yards to a woodlot that bordered the stand of planted pine trees. I began still-hunting through the woods and almost immediately something caught my eye. It was a white set of antlers moving quickly through the woods.

The buck didn't like the high winds any more than I did and was heading for the pines to bed down for the day. I immediately dropped to one knee and whistled loudly several times. The buck eventually stopped dead in his tracks to look over in my direction. Using a nearby tree trunk for a rest, I centered the crosshairs behind the buck's shoulder, and without hesitation, touched off a round.

Adverse weather conditions can dull a buck's primary senses, giving a silent still-hunter a slight advantage. He is still no pushover, however.

The buck bolted for the pines, but he was hit hard in the lungs with a 180-grain Federal Nosler Partition from my Remington pump carbine and he collapsed before he could reach the edge of the hardwoods.

We all dream of hunting deer on quiet frosty mornings and blue-bird autumn afternoons, but some of the best times to chase bucks occurs when the weather is downright nasty. And sometimes the nastier the better!

The reason for this apparent contradiction is simple. Howling winds and heavy precipitation, be it rain, snow, or sleet, tends to dull a buck's primary senses. No longer can they hear you, see you, or even smell you to the degree they are accustomed. Indeed, inclement weather can make them more

Wilderness bucks will often bed near open power lines and beaver dams when winds reach high velocities. The deep woods are too noisy under such conditions.

vulnerable to the astute hunter, especially if that hunter understands the various stages of the rut. Let me explain.

A few years back I was hunting a hardwood ridge late in the afternoon. A cold front was passing through, as evidenced by a sudden drop in temperature and unusually high winds. I thought the deer would be up and feeding early, so I decided to pussyfoot along a stand of nut-bearing oak tress in the hopes of catching a buck off-guard just before darkness fell.

What I found, however, was quite the opposite. The bucks were up and moving about all right, but they were not feeding. Instead, they were running back and forth through the woods as if the devil himself was giving chase. The high winds, approaching 40 miles per hour, were cracking dead branches and whipping saplings around like a scene from a scary Halloween movie.

Because their vision is geared towards picking out moving objects, the deer were being bombarded with images of swaying branches and swirling leaves. That alone was enough to make them quite jittery, but their sense of hearing was also overloaded due to the pop and crackle of tree branches breaking and hitting the ground. Of course, each time a loud snap echoed across the forest, nearby deer would hi-tail it 50 yards or so to safety. Then a dead tree falling to the ground would send them off in another direction. Now, add that confusion to the simple fact their noses could not discriminate subtle odors due to the gushing air currents, and you have several freaked-out bucks cutting back and forth across that ridge for their lives!

Where do bucks go when the winds reach high velocities? Once they have been booted from their usual bedding areas, where the swaying branches and cracking limbs overburden their sensory apparatus, it is not unusual to see farmland deer feeding in open lots in the middle of the day or wilderness bucks bedded around abandoned beaver dams or even along electric power line rights-of-way.

In cattle country, pastures are another good choice to look for bucks on windy days. Once out in the open and away from all the noise, deer will bed down where there is at least some protection from the wind, such as near stone piles, large dead trees, or inside thorn apple thickets to wait out the storm. More than one hunter on his way back to camp has been caught dumbfounded after jumping a trophy buck from such a seemingly unlikely bedding location on a windy morning.

My favorite locations for windy days are abandoned farm fields overgrown with goldenrod, milkweed, Queen Anne's lace, and blackberry briars. Deer like to bed here on slight ridges, near depressions along bordering hedgerows, or next to stands of sumac, where they can stay out of sight but are not bothered as much by the excessive winds.

Sometimes it is best to sit out a storm, especially those tempests that dump a foot or more of snow in deer country.

If there are no open fields, then deer will soon seek refuge in the thickest tangle of brush they can find. Cattail marshes and stands of thick evergreens with branches growing close to the ground are two good choices. Deer will hold tight here despite your intrusion, making it more like a rabbit hunt than a deer hunt.

Indeed, I just about stepped on a 140-class ten-pointer one day in the Adirondacks while blood-trailing a smaller buck hit by another member of our party. The old buck was bedded out of the wind in a stand of small hemlocks below a beaver dam. When he erupted, the commotion so startled me that I jumped backwards, and before I could get my wits about me, he was gone, disappearing forever into the bowels of the swamp.

HEAVY RAINS

Torrential downpours are tough to hunt for any lengthy period of time simply because it is difficult to stay warm and dry on such days. Of course, horizontal rains can also make it difficult for you to see. Nonetheless, these too can be productive times afield if you know where the deer are likely to be. Again, bucks will quickly abandon those locations where they are faced with the brunt of the storm and will seek protection in thick-brush depressions, stands of conifers, patches of mountain laurel, deep ravines, the downwind side of overgrown hedgerows, and, of course, inside uncut corn fields.

However, you will occasionally find whitetails in abandoned fields, old apple orchards, and even wide-open spaces, facing downwind like horses on the range when falling rains meet biblical proportions. With heads drooping, eyes closed shut, and tails tucked tightly between their legs, deer will just stand still, seemingly oblivious to the world as they steadfastly wait out the storm.

One year I walked right up on a mature doe as she hung her head low during an especially heavy thunderstorm. At the time, I thought I could have sneaked in close enough to touch her as she was being pelted with sheet after sheet of white rain. Today I wish I had done so just so I could have seen her come unglued, but at the time I was hoping a buck was bedded down somewhere nearby, so I passed without disturbing her.

RAINY DAYS AND WINDY AFTERNOONS

Still-hunting is the name of the game when high winds and heavy rains prevail. The rain will drown any airborne scent, washing it away in seconds, while heavy winds will just as quickly cover any noise you make. Indeed, you can glide like a ghost through the thickest of vegetation when there is a tempest brewing. These are the days I wade right into the ravines, planted pine

A prolonged rain will soak most ground debris, making it super quiet for still-hunting. This is a good time to sneak around that thick cover you have been avoiding all season long.

plantations, and pockets of thick vegetation in the hopes of jumping a buck at close range. Shots are likely to be up close and personal, so leave your magnum blunderbuss home and opt for a short pump or lever-action instead. You won't regret it.

In this type of weather, you will notice that keeping water droplets off your scope can be a problem. Plastic scope covers can help, but they can also cost you precious seconds when a buck leaps up from behind a blow-down and hightails it across to the opposite ridge. Even clear-plastic scope covers can spoil an otherwise easy shot. The tip-off mounts on my Savage 99 are a good compromise under such conditions while Marlin and Winchester lever-actions fitted with either standard open sights or aftermarket peep sights are also popular. See-through mounts are yet another good choice. Remember, any shot you get is likely to be only 25 to 50 yards distant.

Once the rut kicks into high gear, you have another option when the wind is howling. Despite adverse conditions, the rut will take place, and some bucks will be up and about looking for receptive does no matter what the weather. Still-hunt downwind of bedding areas frequented by family groups of does and fawns, or just inside fingers of brush that protrude into large fields. Both should get their fair share of traffic as the rut nears its peak. Bring your lunch and a thermos and plan on still-hunting all day long despite the weather. It could prove to be one of your most memorable days afield.

One of the best times to still-hunt is during the last few hours of the storm when bucks are more likely to be on the move.

SNOWSTORMS AND WINTER BLIZZARDS

Heavy snowstorms, called nor'easters in my neck of the woods, keep almost everyone holed up in deer camp. But like windstorms and heavy downpours, these too can be productive, even after the rut has peaked. That's because, despite the driven snow, bucks will be moving about looking for one more doe to breed.

The best time to hunt a blizzard is during the last three or four hours of the storm, just as the snow begins to taper off. Bucks will soon start prowling thickets for bedded does, and you can easily pick up their tracks in the freshly fallen snow. This is the weather many experienced snow trackers prefer, as you can follow a single buck's spoor over hill and dale and not lose the trail because it somehow becomes intertwined in other deer tracks.

How do you know you are still-hunting alongside a buck's tracks and not those of a doe? That's easy, actually. Rutting bucks on the prowl do not dilly-dally across the landscape like the does will do once the storm abates. They will trot from one known concentration of does to another. Their trails are more direct and appear as if the buck has a destination in mind.

Upon entering a suspected bedding area, a buck will weave back and forth looking for bedded does, stopping to sniff each bed no matter how old it appears. Once he is satisfied no estrous does are present, he will generally beeline it for the next suspected bedding area.

If you find fresh beds with tracks indicating the deer exited the bed in a hurry, but only ran a short distance, then you might very well be right behind the old boy. The buck probably rousted a doe from her bed to check her breed-

Differentiating doe tracks from the trails of rutting bucks is not all that difficult. One clue: does dillydally, whereas a buck's trail is more purposeful in nature.

ing status, and once convinced she was not in heat, he continued on with his search.

If you are out there, you have a chance of catching up to him. But you have to be out there braving the elements and not back in camp sleeping or playing cards. Howling winds can be a deer hunter's best friend when the weather turns foul!

STAYING PUT DURING THE STORM

Is there ever a time you should stay in camp during periods of stormy weather? Yes, there are two occasions where I generally elect to stay put until the tempest abates. One is during a heavy snowstorm that dumps a foot or more of snow. Driving to your hunting grounds can be dangerous, even with a 4×4. It can also be difficult to walk through the woods, pooping you out in short order. One season it took me two hours to walk a half-mile across an open field. Snowshoes are a real asset under these conditions, but you still have to figure out a way to get your buck out of the woods. And if you are hunting alone in the big woods, that can be a problem.

Pump carbines, open sights, and the absence of a sling are a deadly combination when hunting deep woods whitetails during a snowstorm.

The second occasion I elect to stay in camp is when temperatures plummet to single digits, especially if there are accompanying high winds. Hypothermia and frostbite are real possibilities when these two conditions combine forces.

The main reason I stay out of the woods during periods of heavy snow and frigid temperatures, however, has as much to do with stress as anything else—stress on the deer. Occasionally state organizations will close the deer season when snows get too deep. The deer tend to yard up, and the deep snows keep them in the yard, making them easy targets. And if there was a poor mast crop that autumn and deer are entering the winter in a depleted physical state, the additional stress from hunting can lessen their chances of surviving the upcoming long winter.

Are You Sure You Missed? 22

I almost gave up. It was evident from the several sets of large deer tracks crossing the logging road that a mature buck was passing through this section of the clear-cut on a regular basis. I had prowled the edges of the old cut for three days now without catching ever so much as a fleeting glimpse of him. Nonetheless, I knew the old boy was nearby, and I was determined to wait him out.

Then suddenly, as if on cue, a wide-racked buck materialized in front of me, plodding across the clear-cut some 100 yards distant in a deliberate, "got-to-keep-going" manner. With his head down and neck swollen, it was obvious he was deep in the rut and tired from the rigors of the breeding season. It was also obvious that he would soon disappear behind a thick wall of spruce and mixed fir if I didn't shoot, and shoot quickly.

I dropped to one knee, wrapped the sling around my forearm and peered through the scope. As soon as the crosshairs settled

A solid miss! Until you find such evidence, however, it behooves you to treat every shot as if you scored a direct hit.

on the trailing edge of the buck's left front leg, I touched off a 150-grain pill.

At the sound of my '06, the buck turned around and headed back in the direction from whence he came, showing absolutely no sign of being struck by that bullet. I pumped another shell into the Remington's chamber, but it was too late. The buck had disappeared into the clear-cut as quickly as he had arrived.

I moved quickly, approaching the shooting scene in seconds flat hoping to see the buck lying dead 15 or 20 yards away, but I saw nothing. I scoured the logging road for traces of hair, bone, and blood, but the ground showed no evidence of a hit, nor any sign of the buck's passing, not even his fresh hoof prints. I then dashed out into the clear-cut looking for broken branches, blood—anything that would help me locate that buck, all to no avail. That's when the first traces of doubt entered my brain: Did I miss him? And if I did not, then where did he go?

Each autumn thousands of shots are fired at white-tailed deer. Some deer are shot dead in their tracks while others make good their escape unscathed or with only superficial wounds. Still others are hit, only to die later, never to be found by the hunter.

Adverse weather conditions can play a factor here as can the stamina of the individual animal. Unfortunately, we sometimes lose deer because of our own lack of woodsmanship or tracking abilities. In these cases, we generally think we missed and give up the search way too soon.

Take that wide-racked buck, for example. After searching for tracks, blood, and broken branches only to come up empty-handed, it would have been reasonable for me to assume I had missed the buck. A quick body search in the immediate area the next day would have alleviated any lingering guilt and allowed me to continue my hunt with honor, blaming the scope, the gun, the bullets, my sling, or whatever I could think of for my poor performance under pressure. As it turned out, however, that buck was lying dead less than 100 yards away from where I shot him.

AFTER THE SHOT

Your first responsibility upon firing at a buck is to key all your senses onto his reaction to the shot and his attempts to escape. Often a buck will kick his rear legs out, hunch his back, stumble, run flat-out, or even fall right down only to get right back up again, indicating a probable hit. However, he might instead turn around and run, retracing his earlier steps with his tail tucked tightly between his legs. Or he might run straight away from you while waving his white flag back and forth like a pendulum on a clock. In each of these cases,

Often, but not always, a buck will kick like a mule, hunch his back, or run flat out, indicating a probable hit.

you might have made a killing shot even though the buck with the flashy tail acted as if you missed him clean.

I once had a buck bound away as if I shot harmlessly over his back. Upon reflection, however, I remembered seeing water spray off the buck's shoulder, so I continued looking for him despite my lack of confidence in my shooting skills. I eventually found the buck, and that spray turned out to be the point of entry of the 12-gauge slug from my Ithaca Deerslayer.

In addition to watching the deer carefully, you must also keep your ears wide open, cupping one if necessary in an effort to pinpoint the buck's exact escape route. In some cases, you can actually trail a wounded buck quite a distance in this manner, giving you important clues to his eventual whereabouts in the absence of blood splatters and scuffed-up leaves. Indeed, bucks make noises when they ford streams, scurry up steep hillsides, jump barbed wire fences, and crawl over stone walls. They even sometimes stop in mid-stride to change routes, leaving precious little sign to point you in the right direction.

Several seasons ago I rifled a decent Montana buck as he exited a cattail swamp. Common sense told me the buck escaped back into the cattails, but then I remembered the only sound I heard after the shot was a slight rustling of leaves, not the crashing one would expect to hear from a buck on his death

This is a good blood trail. You can also trail a buck by listening for the noises it makes as it jumps barbed-wire fences or crosses streams.

march through the swamp. I soon located that buck dead as a rock 10 yards outside the marsh. I learned then that it always pays to keep your ears open after the shot.

LOCATION, LOCATION, LOCATION

Once things settle down, you must mark the spot where the buck stood at the shot, and where you last saw or heard him after the shot. Use plenty of detail here, such as a fallen log, a scarred-up old tree, or even an off-color pile of leaves to help you mark the exact locations.

Just as important, you must also mark the spot from where you took the shot. You may be surprised to learn how difficult it is to retrace the events if you cannot go back to the shooting scene. You may also be surprised to learn how difficult it is to return to that shooting scene unless you mark it somehow *before* you go to look for your buck. I invariably hang my hat or wrap a handkerchief around a nearby limb as soon as things settle down after the shooting. Only then do I carefully move towards the spot where the buck was standing when I shot.

Take this wide-racked buck, for example. I picked out two distinct landmarks to help me find where the buck was standing when I shot and where I last saw him after the shot, and I left my backpack at the shooting scene before I went looking for him. Good thing, too, for I had to return to the shooting scene three or four times to help find the buck's tracks, which were barely visible on the shoulder of that old logging road.

Locating his tracks that afternoon was an important piece of information, especially since I could not find any blood or hair at the scene. I eventually got down on my hands and knees and from that angle could then easily see where the buck re-entered the clear-cut. A faint odor of musk seemed to confirm my suspicions. Then, with the discovery of some slightly crushed vegetation in

Mark the spot from which you shot and the last place you saw him before he disappeared from view before picking up his blood trail. You may need to retrace your steps should you lose the trail.

the clear-cut, it was easy to follow his escape route for 30 yards or so before it petered out.

I then realized that the light bullet I was using might not have passed completely through the buck (I now favor a 180-grain or heavier bullet when hunting big-bodied northern whitetails), which might account for the absence of any kind of blood trail. I also realized that with the absence of blood, I might have indeed missed him clean, which meant that the buck was probably long gone. Or I could have gut shot him, which would really complicate matters.

NEVER GIVE UP

Many hunters would have felt comfortable giving up right then and there. And I almost did. Instead, I went back to the last broken branch and conducted a "blood-or-body" search in a 50-yard arc. Over the years I have stumbled upon many a lost buck in such a manner. It is astonishing how small a buck is when he is lying on his side and even more astonishing how close you can get to him before you realize that he is dead.

One year I was tracking a bow-shot eight-pointer of mine that I was sure ran full-bore across a grown-over field. There was a faint blood trail, but it

It is amazing how small a big buck can be when he is curled up dead in the weeds. Don't look for the whole deer when doing a body search but rather for a glint of antler or a white belly.

suddenly quit only 10 yards or so from where I shot the buck. I continued on down the game trail the buck was using as an escape route but could not locate any more sign, so I returned to the last speck of blood and casually looked around. A white spot caught my eye, but I quickly dismissed it. A few minutes later that white spot caught my eye again. This time I looked more carefully. You guessed it; my buck had died on his feet less than 20 yards from where I shot him. The arrow had severed the aorta, and he had simply veered off the game trail and fell over dead.

What is the moral of this story? Bucks don't always travel great distances before expiring. Indeed, I have found dead bucks curled up in brush piles, floating in creeks, and bloated up in the thickest, nastiest tangles. I have also had bucks double back on their own tracks before falling over dead. And each time, they were located not too far from the last splatter of blood or last scuffed-up leaf.

In the case of my wide-racked buck, I went back and did another quick body search, but I was overwhelmed. The clear-cut was huge, and if the buck was indeed dead, he could be lying anywhere. I even checked the logging road again in case the buck doubled back after the shot, but I could not find any sign.

TRUST YOUR SHOOTING SKILLS

This is the point in time where you must relive the shot over and over again in your mind. Where were the crosshairs when you squeezed the trigger? Did you in fact touch one off, or did you panic and jerk the trigger? Were you holding steady on target? Did you factor in the forward movement of the buck? Did you calculate the actual shooting distance correctly? Finally, are you confident you did not miss and instead shot a bull's-eye?

As I relived the shot over and over again, I came to realize that I had indeed killed that deer. I had dropped to a kneeling position and used my sling to help steady my rifle. I picked a spot to shoot at before I raised my rifle, and when the crosshairs settled in on target, I carefully squeezed the trigger, surprising myself when the gun went off. Yes, I knew I killed that deer, but where was he?

I remembered there was a brook about 150 yards from the logging road. If the buck made it that far, there should be some sign indicating where he crossed the water. Any broken branches, wet leaves, or fresh splayed tracks here would tell me he had made it to the stream, but there was not so much as an old deer track anywhere along the creek.

I went back one more time to the logging road to retrace my steps. When I came to the end of the trail, I decided to continue on in the same direction by taking the easiest and most obvious route. I hadn't gone 20 yards or so when I caught another whiff of musk. Suddenly it hit me. That was the same odor I had caught wind of earlier. Could this be the clue I was looking for?

If the shot felt good, be relentless in your search. If he died nearby, you'll find him.

The end of the trail. I had not missed as I feared but rather made a perfect shot.

I put my nose to work and carefully threaded my way through the brush and fir trees until I came upon a fat, wide-racked, 250-pound wilderness buck lying dead on his side, his 21-plus-inch rack almost completely concealed by thick vegetation. In fact, I nearly stepped on him and could have easily walked by him in the thick undergrowth without even catching a glimpse of him; he was that well hidden.

I picked up the rack and was surprised to learn he didn't have any brow tines, but I didn't care. The buck had expired in mid-stride with a single bullet hole low and behind the right shoulder. Not only had I not missed, I had made a perfect shot. What else could I ask for?

Blood-Trailing Marginally Hit Bucks | 23

Following up on marginal hits is the burden of every deer hunter. It's called responsibility.

The tracks in the snow told the story. From the looks of things, a yearling deer—I couldn't tell yet if it was a buck or a doe—was working its way along the lee side of the cliff. It was going quite slow, dragging a rear leg, I surmised, and feeding nonchalantly along the way. The trail was smoking hot, but I wasn't interested in shooting a yearling Adirondack deer, so I wasn't ready when the six-point raised his head a mere 20 yards away for a casual look around.

His eyes flashed past me without notice, and the buck continued picking his way through the brush growing along the face of the cliff. I decided to follow him a ways, just to see where he was going, when I noticed a few red droplets of blood in his track that weren't there initially. Another hunter in camp had taken a shot at a yearling buck a few days earlier, hitting it in the right rear leg he thought, but was unable to recover it.

I wondered, could this be that buck? Suddenly, the wind changed and the buck bolted away, but not before I saw his right rear leg flopping back and forth like a rag in the breeze. I snapped off a shot, hoping to put the cripple down, but the bullet from my '06 only grazed his hindquarters.

Committed to taking the animal if I could, I gave chase. The trail was easy to follow, as the leg wound had opened up, spilling fresh red blood atop the new snow like it came from a spray gun. The buck never gave up, and for the next hour or so, it was an even foot race until I finally caught up to him in the thick laurel and finished him off with a single shot to the neck. I learned later that the six-point was indeed the buck the other hunter had shot at earlier in the week.

SURVIVOR BUCKS

Blood-trailing a marginally hit deer, one whose injuries are not immediately fatal, is often an iffy proposition. If the blood trail is sparse and just peters out after a hundred yards, or worse, seems to go on for miles and miles, the hunter is forced to make a decision. Should he stay on the trail or give up the chase? And if he does turn around and go home, will the buck survive the season or curl up and die in some thicket days later?

This buck lost his lower leg, maybe due to a hunting incident or car accident. Notice how well it healed over. The buck walked with a definite limp but was still capable of strong bursts of speed.

Well, bucks do survive marginal hits, but not always. Unless a major blood vessel is severed, muscle wounds usually heal up rather quickly, although life-threatening infections can set in on occasion. Liver hits are usually fatal, but it may take the animal four to eight hours or more to succumb to the wound. And gut-shot deer sometimes survive, although rarely, while deer shot in either the front or rear leg quite often survive if there are adequate food supplies and few predators.

Every other summer or so, I stumble upon a buck that seems to have survived the winter despite a serious wound to the leg. It always amazes me how well fed the animal seems to be despite one limb being

Replay the shot over and over in your head before you begin looking for signs of a hit. Did the buck duck the shot or did you see water spray off his hide at the point of impact?

out of commission. They may hobble a bit, especially when feeding, but otherwise they appear perfectly healthy.

One buck in particular was a fine two- or three-and-a-half-year-old eight-pointer that seemed to favor one of his front legs. The bruiser pushed the scales around 200 pounds live weight, but probably due to his injury, he sported a rather odd-looking rack. One side was grotesquely lopsided, which would definitely keep him out of any of the record books, but he was still a magnificent animal. As I watched him feed one evening, I thought how easy it would be to run that buck down Indian-style, until something spooked him and I saw him quickly hightail it back to thick cover. Sure, he favored one leg, but he could still outrun me with ease, and any four-legged predators in the neighborhood, too!

Does this mean that marginally hit deer are rarely recoverable? Absolutely not! Here's how to increase your chances of tagging a buck shot in the leg, liver, or paunch.

AFTER THE SHOT

Blood-trailing a marginally hit deer should begin right after you touch off a round. What you do in the next few minutes often spells the difference between recovering that animal or kicking yourself for blowing the shot.

After you mark your exact shooting location but before you run over and look for blood, play the whole shooting incident over in your mind a couple of times. Where was the buck standing when the gun went off? Where were the crosshairs? Were they rock steady or wavering about? Did you squeeze off a shot or did you jerk the trigger? What was the buck's reaction to the shot? Did he vamoose as if you missed him clean? Did he kick his feet up like a mule? Did he hunch his back? Did he run close to the ground? Did you see where the bullet struck the animal? Did you see a tuft of hair explode off his hide? If it had been raining, did you see water spray off his hide? Did you hear the bullet strike something hard, like bone? Did the buck slow down before he ran out of sight, even down to a walk?

Don't let a leg-shot buck rest or "stiffen up" as conventional wisdom so often dictates; give immediate chase instead.

After reflecting on the shot, it's time to examine the last spot the buck was standing when you pulled the trigger to see if there is snow on the ground, blood, hair, bits of bones, and, of course, his tracks should be easy to find. If not, you may have to get down on your hands and knees to examine the site very carefully. Mark each bit of sign with orange flagging tape as you go along. This will help you determine his line of travel should the blood sign become sparse.

Generally speaking, if you find evidence of a hit but don't find your buck down for the count within 200 yards, you can bet your last bullet you probably have a marginally hit buck. Your job now is to determine where the animal is wounded and react accordingly.

LEG WOUNDS

A buck shot in either leg often exits the scene with an unusual gait. You might see blood on the leg, or you might see him hop, skip, or leap forward as he attempts to make good his escape. You might even see the leg flopping back and forth. There should also be plenty of bright red blood on one side of the trail, the side the bullet hit, at least initially. If you follow the trail long enough, you will find where the buck bedded down, and you will see more blood in the bed.

What are your options? Well, conventional wisdom often tells us to sit down on a log for a half-hour or so to wait for the buck to either bleed to death or "stiffen up," allowing him to be easily approached for the final blow. What usually happens when the buck is left alone, however, is that he does indeed bed down but does not bleed to death. Instead, the wound clots, and if not disturbed by other hunters or predators, nature takes its course. The buck may lose the wounded portion of the leg, or it may heal, leaving him with a limp. In any event, the buck can survive.

Your best chance of recovering a buck shot in the leg is to pursue the animal with vigor. Get a friend or two and track him down purposely and relentlessly, an easier task if there is snow on the ground. Without the white stuff, however, blood and scuffed-up leaves should give you enough clues as to the buck's immediate whereabouts. It should be agreed upon beforehand that the buck be finished off at the first opportunity by anybody in the party. Otherwise, you might be chasing that buck for the better part of the day, and in some cases, into the next.

LIVER HITS

The liver is located in the upper middle of the body between the buck's lungs and paunch. How do you know you have hit a deer in the liver? If you can imagine a buck standing broadside, then the angle of your bullet's entry should give you a clue. The presence of dark red blood, however, is a dead give-away. It usually indicates you missed the lungs and caught the liver instead.

The most common mistake deer hunters make recovering a liver-shot deer is to immediately begin tracking the deer down. Unless a main blood vessel was

Liver shots and paunch hits are best left undisturbed for several hours. Go back to camp, dry off, get something to eat, and return later that day or the next morning.

severed, causing the deer to expire quickly, the buck will jump up from his bed when you get too close and vacate the scene, leaving a scant blood trail for you to follow. The buck will then travel for up to several hundred yards before bedding down again, and unless there is ample snow on the ground, you probably will not find him.

The rule of thumb is to wait at least four to six hours (with eight hours even better) before picking up the trail of a liver-shot deer. If you wait the proper length of time, you should find where your buck bedded down and expired within 150 yards of where you shot him.

PAUNCH

If you think you hit the buck a little too far back, then you probably shot him in the stomach. How do you know that for sure? The buck may act as if nothing is wrong as he scampers away to thick cover, leaving you to wonder if you might have missed him altogether. More often, however, he kicks his hind legs high like a mule and then simply bounds off for 50 or 60 yards. He then stops in his tracks, hunches his back, and moves slowly away with an awkward stiff-legged gait. You can confirm your suspicions by examining the shooting site for bits of partially digested food or tufts of white belly hair. There may even be a strong odor of feces in the air.

If you pursue a gut-shot buck, he may travel several hundred yards before lying up, leaving little or no blood trail to betray his whereabouts. A body search may be your only option then.

The problem with gut-shot deer is two-fold. One, fat and intestines usually plug the entry and exit holes, stopping any slow-dripping blood from reaching the ground. Thus, the blood trail may start out promising but soon peter out to just an occasional drop. And secondly, gut-shot deer can live for several hours after the incident, often traveling 100 to 300 yards and bedding down several times before expiring.

As in the liver shot, the biggest mistake hunters make is picking up the blood trail too soon after the shot. If you suspect you have a gut-shot animal, the wise course is to quietly remove yourself from the scene and wait at least twelve hours before blood trailing. Waiting overnight is never a bad idea. Your buck won't be any more dead the next morning than he would be several hours after the shot.

Your other option is to keep the deer in sight all day long by being stealthy and by using your binoculars. As noted above, a deer hit in

Knowing when to sit tight and when to push hard on marginal hits can spell the difference between success and failure in the deer woods.

the paunch will bed down several times before expiring, and since there is often little or no blood trail, staying just within sight of him can be a wise strategy. Indeed, more than one gut-shot deer has stood up after lying down all morning long only to wander off and never be seen again. Any disturbance, be it man or beast, can spook your buck, causing him to sneak several hundred yards away to hide in a swamp, standing corn lot, or thorn-apple thicket deep into your neighbor's property. Your chances of recovering that buck then are very slim indeed.

As you can see, some deer do survive marginal hits while others run off and die without ever being recovered. The path to success is to look for clues, pay attention to detail, and then let logic take its course.

24 Shooting Tips That Will Save Your Season

If you want to consistently shoot bucks on the prowl, then you have to have a few tricks up your sleeve.

Let's face the facts. Most of us only get a few days each season to bag a buck. Demands at work and home keep us out of the woods more than we would like, limiting not only our pre-season scouting time but also the number of hours we can actually be afield.

Knowing that we might only get one opportunity to shoot can put an excessive amount of pressure on us, and that one opportunity may not offer us a high-percentage shot. In fact, when the moment of truth presents itself, we better be ready to shoot and shoot accurately, perhaps under the worst of conditions, or go home empty-handed.

Over the years, I have missed my share of bucks. Sometimes I shot too soon while at other times I waited too long and never fired a round. Other times, I simply fevered up and missed racked bucks by the proverbial country mile.

But I didn't miss them all. Over the past forty-five years or so, I have connected on a wealth of deer, including several tall-tined beauties that now hang in my den. Not all of them were classic shots, however; some were one-of-a-kind doozies that still bring a smile to my face. Indeed, over the years I have learned that if you want to consistently shoot bucks, you have to have a few tricks up your sleeve. Here are a few my friends and I use to help us shoot straight and true.

REALISTIC PRACTICE

Each fall I watch hunters at the target range sight-in their guns. Invariably there are always a few nimrods who insist on standing up to shoot off-hand at bull's-eye targets 100 yards distant. If one out of four or five rounds hits somewhere near the center of the target, they are satisfied with the results. Then they rattle off a full clip in rapid succession, for the heck of it, I suppose, before casing their guns, content in the false belief they are ready for deer season.

To be a dead shot in the deer woods, you must first practice at unknown yardages from unorthodox positions. Bull's-eyes on the rifle range don't count.

Once in a while they might shoot a deer, but by and large, these guys spray the woods at the first sight of a deer without ever drawing blood, and then blame the gun, the scope, the ammo, or whatever else for missing. Truth is, their guns were never sighted properly in the first place, and in the second place, they never practiced correctly.

Shooting from a solid rest at the gun range is only the first step in preparing your deer slayer for the upcoming opener. Conventional wisdom tells us that pie-plate-size groups at 100 yards is adequate on deer-sized game, but groups the size of your fist—or smaller—are what you are really looking for. The tighter the groups the more leeway you have in the field when the moment of truth arrives.

But accuracy at the bench does not guarantee accuracy in the woods. Not by a long shot. To be a dead shot in the deer woods, you must be able to hit whitetails at unknown yardages from unorthodox positions. And the best way to gain this kind of accuracy is to make your practice sessions as realistic as possible. A ravine filled with deer-size targets will help you gain the perspective you need and will teach you that shooting from the prone position is more accurate than shooting free-hand standing up, and that sitting or kneeling is also deadly—especially if you employ a log, mound of dirt, or a tree trunk as a rest.

PROPER SIGHTING SYSTEMS

Most of us hunt with scoped rifles or shotguns these days. But a telescopic sight is not always the best system in the deer woods. Even a low-power model can cause problems when hunting the thick stuff or during a heavy storm.

Veteran outdoor writer Ken Allen once told me about a survey conducted in his home state of Maine. It indicated that on bluebird days, most trophy bucks destined for the Maine Skull and Antler Trophy Club were tagged by hunters using scoped rifles, but during periods of heavy precipitation, peep sights ruled.

New York state guide Mark Eddy echoes these findings, but with a slight twist. "See-through mounts and tip-off mounts are very popular in the mountains," explains Eddy. "For similar reasons peep sights are tops during inclement weather in Maine. We get a lot of snow here, and whether you are still-hunting or tracking, an opportunity can come and go in a matter of sec-

Choose a sight system that gets you on target fast under current weather conditions.

onds, offering you precious little time to wipe the moisture from your scope. Even if it is not snowing or raining, a buck can appear in front of you only a few scant yards away, making it difficult to find him quickly in the scope. This is where the two-sight system of see-through or tip-off mounts really shines."

THE RIGHT GUN FOR THE JOB

There are lots of ways to kill a whitetail. You can stalk bucks on the open prairie, still-hunt them along river bottoms and hardwood ridges, ambush one from a tree-stand set up in the thick stuff, or simply post near a game trail. All are proven techniques, but to maximize your odds of making an accurate shot, you need to use the right gun for the job. Let me explain.

A long-barreled bolt-action magnum fitted with a tripod and high-power variable scope may just be the ideal weapon when hunting whitetails on the prairie or along gas-line and power-line rights-of-way where 200- to 300-yard shots are common enough, but it is not

Maximize your odds by choosing the right gun and caliber according to terrain features and weather conditions.

the weapon of choice for still-hunting through thick swamps and hardwood ridges where shots average 50 to 75 yards. A carbine fitted with open sights or a low-power variable would prove more deadly. My .30-06 Remington pump carbine fitted with a low-power variable scope is just the ticket here, and in fact, it is one of the top three most popular deer rifles in the Northeast.

Of course, if there is inclement weather and you are trying to slip through brushy hillsides, a lever-action fitted with a peep sight, like my Model 94 Winchester chambered for the brutal .356 Win Mag, is definitely the better choice. My backup is a vintage Model 99 Savage in .300 Savage fitted with a fixed low-power Weaver scope and tip-off mounts.

A pump carbine topped with a low-power variable is one of the top three deer rifles in the Northeast.

The moral here is clear. Tailor the gun, caliber, and sight system to your hunting terrain and current weather conditions and you will shoot more bucks.

FREE HANDS

A rut-crazed buck can appear out of nowhere at any time of the day, so you must be prepared to shoot him at a moment's notice. And that means ditching the bulky gloves and snowmobile mittens. It simply takes too much time to remove these heavy hand warmers in time to make the shot.

Several seasons back, I was still-hunting along a big-woods scrape line when I caught a buck flatfooted while working the line in my direction. The temperatures were in the single digits that morning, and I had a thick pair of insulated mittens on to help keep my fingers from freezing. I saw the buck first, but the mittens were so thick I could not grasp the trigger. I bit the tip and used my teeth to pull the mitten free, but when it dropped to the ground, the buck caught the movement and skedaddled before I could take aim.

Whenever I am still-hunting today, I try to wear a pair of thin cotton or wool gloves that allow me to flick off the safety and make the killing shot with ease. When temperatures drop to intolerable levels, however, an insulated muff packed with hand warmers helps keep my gloved hands toasty warm while still allowing me to shoot at a moment's notice.

KEEP THE RECEIVER FROM FREEZING

On days of extremely cold temperatures, it is possible to have your rifle's receiver actually freeze solid, prohibiting you from taking any shot. The firing pin will simply not drop. Jim Massett, past president of the New York State Big Buck Club, is one of the top deer hunters in the East who specializes in tracking bucks down in the snow. Over the years, he has trailed dozens and

Ditch those heavy gloves and mittens, and keep your hands free to fire at a moment's notice.

To stop your receiver from freezing solid, carry your rifle with your hand wrapped around the receiver. A frozen firing pin won't drop!

dozens of bucks to their doom, many when temperatures were downright nasty.

"It can be very frustrating to finally get the drop on a buck you've been chasing all day only to have the gun fail to go off," says Massett. "I carry my rifle with my hand wrapped around the receiver to help keep it from freezing up. It can be awkward at times, and some models like the Winchester and Marlin lever-actions are easier to tote in this fashion than others, but it is one of those tricks that generally separates the casual deer hunter from the real woodsmen."

HANG UP THE SLING

Another secret tactic used by veteran buck hunters involves the sling. That is, they don't use it while hunting. Carrying your rifle over your shoulder while snow tracking, or sneaking and peeking, is a recipe for disaster.

I learned this lesson the hard way one season when I came upon a nice eight-pointer working a hardwood ridge in my direction. I saw him first, but the extra movement involved in un-slinging my pump and then bringing it to my shoulder caught the buck's wary eye. He hitailed it back along the ridge before I could center the crosshairs.

Some hunters remove the sling and stuff it in a fanny pack for the duration of the hunt. I leave my sling attached, however, in case I need it for support later on. I recently used my sling to help steady my '06 on a 170-yard shot at a twelve-pointer. The buck was walking slowly and there was no rest nearby. I wrapped my arm into the sling and made the shot from a sitting position.

Get in the habit of carrying your rifle at port arms, not slung over your shoulder. If need be, ditch the sling.

TRACKING

This next blunder taught me how to move through the woods undetected, be it with bow, rifle, or muzzleloader. It also improved my tracking skills. Indeed, you use many of the same skills still-hunting as you do snow tracking big-woods bucks.

About twenty-five years ago, I was gun hunting Vermont's opening week when I came upon a set of wide-splayed tracks in the still-falling snow. A single deer had crossed a tote road, zigzagged through a belt of brush that ringed the valley, and then headed straight up into the high country.

I immediately began trailing the deer, and judging by the amount of fresh snow in the tracks, he was only ten or fifteen minutes in front of me. Nonetheless, I rushed forward with youthful enthusiasm, hoping to get a crack at him at any moment.

The trail led up the hill and then through an opening in the forest. I peered across the flat, and not seeing a standing deer looking back at me, trekked brazenly across the meadow.

The buck, however, was standing on the far side checking his back trail when I entered the opening. I can still see the dark-horned mountain buck

You use the same skills still-hunting as you do snow tracking racked deer.

hightail out of sight with a series of great twenty-foot leaps. I struggled to find him in my sights, but it was to no avail. Alas, the buck was gone for good.

I learned from that encounter to never cross an opening in plain view. Instead, I now travel through the woods like a deer by sticking to the shadows and by taking advantage of terrain features and available vegetation. Move about so you can see but not be seen.

TAKE THE FIRST GOOD SHOT

Deer camps are full of stories about ghost-like bucks that drifted back into brush never to be seen again. When you press for details, however, you learn that in many cases the hunter had an opportunity at the buck but waited for a closer shot or better angle. Or he thought he had more time to assess the situation only to have the buck turn and saunter out of sight.

Such was the case several seasons ago. It was early in the pre-rut, and I was still-hunting with my '06 along the flats of the Bull River in western Montana where a friend had seen a huge 150-class whitetail the previous week. A series of rubs and scrape lines indicated this particular buck's preferred morning hangout, and I was there to see if I could intercept the big ten-pointer before he headed into the high country to bed down.

I was about ready to give up around 10 o'clock that frosty morning when I heard something moving across the hillside about 125 yards in front of me. I immediately spotted a deer as it passed broadside to me through an opening in the trees and then stopped partially concealed behind a blow-down. I quickly raised my Swarovski 8x30s for a better look-see and was amazed at the size of the deer's body. I also noticed dark, black splotches at the hock on the inside of his hind legs, although I did not recognize them for what they were until later that day.

I knew it was a deer, in fact a mature buck, although I hadn't seen his rack yet. The mistake I made right then and there was not immediately raising my rifle. Sure, it could have been a small-racked deer, but I thought I had time to study the rack with my binoculars before I brought my gun to bear. I was wrong!

The buck suddenly walked between two trees, giving me one quick look at his tall tines. Then he turned and disappeared into the brush. It was the 150-class ten-pointer, and if I had my rifle shouldered, I would have had four or five seconds to line up the crosshairs and squeeze off a shot. More than enough time! The worse part was that I never saw that buck again, and again, I went home with a clean tag.

Today, as soon as I verify what I am looking at is indeed a deer, I throw my gun up and peer through the scope. It only takes a fraction of a second then to push the safety off, line up the crosshairs, and shoot. I don't waste precious time. Once I am sure I am looking at a deer, I use my scope to assess the rack—not my binoculars.

If you have a killing shot, take it. Waiting for an even better angle could cost you the shot.

PICK A SPOT AND STICK WITH IT

This boo-boo still smarts because I missed the heaviest buck I ever caught flat-footed in the big woods. I was still-hunting along a New Brunswick scrape line, a favorite tactic of mine, when I caught a glimpse of a heavy-bodied behemoth checking each scrape and making rubs. A line of alders prevented me from taking a shot right then and there, but he was about to cross a grown-over logging road, offering me a clean shot through a small window of opportunity.

When the buck stepped into the opening, I centered the crosshairs on his neck, but at the last moment, I decided to push a projectile into his lungs instead. I lowered the crosshairs a bit, but to my chagrin had some trouble dis-

Don't second-guess yourself. Choose a sight picture before you raise your rifle, and stick with it.

tinguishing them against the buck's dark body. I touched off a round and the buck leaped up into the air and then sprinted off into the bush.

Confident I had a solid hit, I slowly worked my way over to where the buck last stood. I had hit him all right, as evidenced by a few tufts of hair and a faint bright blood trail. But that trail petered out almost immediately, and after a couple of hours of searching on my hands and knees, I concluded that I had only grazed the brisket on that 375-pound buck, and that he was none the worse for the encounter.

The lesson here is simple. You must pick a spot to shoot at and have the desired sight picture in mind before you raise your rifle to shoot. Changing the sight picture at the last second is a sure recipe for disaster.

TAKE THAT EXTRA SECOND

A crack shot always takes that extra second to find a suitable rest before squeezing off a round and avoids shooting off-hand whenever possible. This takes practice, patience, and confidence in your shooting skills.

All too often, though, the hunter gets excited and fears the buck will step out of view, so he gets off one or two shots as fast as possible, hoping one of them will connect. Those hunters who practiced realistically know better, however, and after securing a solid rest, take a deep breath, center the crosshairs, exhale, and drop the buck. Don't rush that shot!

CAP HIM TWICE

We have all heard stories about bucks that suddenly came alive in the bed of someone's pickup, jumped out, and ran back into the woods, apparently none the worse for the encounter.

Well, it happens more often than you think. The buck may not jump out of a truck, but he will suddenly get back on his feet upon your initial approach, even if mortally wounded, and make good his escape.

I have had this happen to me twice, and both times I was flabbergasted. Fortunately, on each occasion I was able to shoot again and drop the buck while he was in flight. These experiences taught me to treat every buck as if he were still alive and shoot him again upon my final approach. And pay extra attention to those bucks lying flat on their stomachs with their heads resting on their chins! Bullets are cheap when compared to a lost animal.

Don't rush your shot. You have more time than you think, and it only takes a split second to do it right.

Bullets are cheap. If you are not sure the buck is dead, shoot him again or he may disappear from your life forever.

Never pass up a buck on opening day you would be more than happy to tag on the last day.

WATCH WHAT YOU PASS UP

Even good hunters can blow a season, especially those that are trophy hunting. For the want of a better buck, we allow lesser animals to walk past without firing a shot. This most often occurs on guided hunts where a lot of money has been spent in the hopes of bringing home a real wall-hanger.

One season in Montana I decided not to squeeze off a shot at a very nice deer, a huge non-typical, because the outfitter had told me an even bigger buck had been seen several times in the immediate vicinity. Well, guess what? That non-typical was the big buck in question, and I never did see him again. I ended my hunt that year with a 120-class ten-pointer, and I was lucky to get him. Big bucks don't get big by being stupid, and that non-typical, feeling the pressure of my presence opening day, left the area for the remainder of the season.

What's the moral here? As I advised bowhunters earlier, never pass up any deer on opening day that you would be more than happy to shoot on the last day! And that advice, my friends, will save any deer season.

First Blast! 25

Follow this old logging road for about a mile and a half," I explained to Will, "until you come to a steep descent. There's an old apple orchard halfway down the ridge on your left and an abandoned homestead complete with cellar hole and more apple trees farther down the hill and off to your right. Bucks cross back and forth along the straightaway here, so stay alert; it's a good spot."

Edwards aimed his flashlight at the topo and then nodded in agreement. "It looks like there is a creek at the bottom of the hill. It also looks like the logging road splits on the other side, with the right fork edging along the swamp. I'll hunt the farmstead until 10 or 11 o'clock and then meet you where the road crosses the creek. I should have my buck by the time we rendezvous."

I tried not to laugh at Will's deadpan delivery. After all, we were hunting the early muzzle-loader season in the heart of the Adirondacks. Sure, the area held

Many states now offer an early season for blackpowder buffs. For states like New York, these hunts take place in wilderness areas just when the leaves are turning crimson, orange, and yellow.

some gnarly old bucks, but this is the big woods and deer aren't as plentiful here as they are in rich farm country.

Nonetheless, we gathered our daypacks and headed off into the darkness. First light was still way off, and we wanted to be in prime deer country before the sun rose. The skidder trail soon forked near the top of the first ridge. We stopped there for a breather then wished each other luck before splitting up. The plan was for me to work my through the beech ridges, drop down to the creek, and then swing north along the swamp towards the abandoned homestead.

It was a bit frosty, and the dead leaves underfoot crackled like spilled cornflakes on the kitchen floor. I wasn't too concerned about the noise, however, as I figured the rising sun would soon melt the frost, leaving the leaves damp for a few hours—perfect still-hunting conditions.

Will wasn't concerned about the dead leaves, either. He stayed on the logging road, still-hunting slowly along the edges where he could be deathly quiet. His strategy paid off within twenty minutes of shooting light when he heard a couple of deer crashing through the dry leaves near the old homestead. When a buck stepped out onto the logging road, Edwards raised his Knight Revolution, aimed a little high through the Burris scope, and sent a Hornady sabot hurling in its direction. The tall-tined six-point bucked at the 210-yard effort and then raced across the old logging road with his tail tucked tightly between his legs. His desperate dash for safety was to no avail, though, as the old buck was already dead on his feet, dropping to the ground a short distance away with a perfect lung shot.

"I told you I'd have a buck by the time you showed up," Will said with that vacant look on his face. I couldn't stifle my laughter this time as I shook my head in disbelief. A big-woods buck in twenty minutes! After hearing the details of the shot and admiring the gnarly twisted rack, we each grabbed a main beam and started the arduous five-hour drag back to my waiting 4×4.

One of the most overlooked opportunities deer hunters have today is rack hunting during an early blackpowder season. Most of these hunts take place in wilderness regions, where deer numbers and the number of deer hunters are both low, generally just a few per square mile of habitat. The odds of you dumping a trophy buck may be tough in these regions, but the odds of you bumping into another human being are slim, too, giving those hunters who are looking for more than a punched tag the opportunity for a quality deer hunting experience.

In my home state of New York, sections of the Adirondack Mountains— with its hundreds of square miles of wilderness habitat—open up to blackpowder enthusiasts just as the leaves are turning crimson, orange, and yellow.

Bucks are in prime condition now, and there is a nip in the air. Indeed, there is no finer time to be afield!

EARLY-SEASON FOOD SOURCES

Of course, locating a buck or two in the deep woods is no easy task, especially if you have been chasing bucks around your uncle's farm all your life. The key in the early season is to zero in on prime food sources, especially mast such as acorns, beechnuts, and apples. You will need to hoof it about and do some pre-season scouting to locate ripe stands of beech and oak, as these trees do not produce every year. Apples, on the other hand, are a much more reliable food source from one season to the next, if you can locate the trees.

This is where a topographical map can come in handy. Orchards on the fringe of the big woods show up as three or four rows of green squiggly circles, each circle representing a tree. The orchards for which you are looking lie deep in the woods near old farmsteads. It seems in years past every farm had a tree or two growing nearby. You won't find the trees on the topo, but you can often locate the old farmsteads. Look

The secret to finding early-season bucks is food, but don't overlook the sudden appearance of the season's first scrapes and scrape lines. They, too, can help you get a line on a buck.

for jeep trails and unimproved roads that dead-end in the middle of nowhere, and then look for a couple of black boxes indicating a nearby cluster of buildings. You will have to scout the area thoroughly to confirm your suspicions, but over the years, I have found several abandoned farmland orchards in this manner that still attract whitetails. And best of all, I generally have these hot spots all to myself!

Water also attracts wilderness bucks like the proverbial moth to a flame. River bottoms, creek beds, swamps, ponds, and the inlets and outlets to larger lakes can also be found on your topographical maps. Water, of course, is printed in blue.

I pay particularly close attention to steep ridges and plateaus above these waterways in addition to gentle slopes that offer easy crossing routes from one side to the other. These can be killer still-hunting routes, especially if there is mast or other food sources nearby.

What you won't find on topo maps, however, are beaver dams. "Bucks often bed in the thick cover below the dam and use the dams as conduits to get from one side to the other," says Adirondack guide Mark Eddy. "If the dam has been breached, bucks will also feed on the new growth above the dam. Forest rangers, game wardens, biologists, and local trappers can sometimes help you locate hidden beaver flows. A quick walk-around will soon tell you if bucks are in the vicinity."

Clear-cuts, burns, slides, avalanches, and blow-downs, as well as power lines, gas lines, and other rights-of-way, open up the forest canopy to sunlight, and hence new growth. Those openings that are two to eight years old seem to attract and hold the most deer. The trick now is to view these openings as nothing more than large agricultural fields. Bucks will enter and exit here in the corners, along creek bottoms, fingers of brush, and anywhere else there is ample cover.

EARLY-SEASON STRATEGIES

The most popular big-woods strategy is undoubtedly still-hunting. The cornerstone to tagging a buck while still-hunting, however, is seeing him before he sees you, which is not always an easy task, considering the type of cover to which bucks are attracted. And the practice is made all the more difficult by the manner in which we hunters usually walk—we like to constantly watch where our feet are going. The real trick to still-hunting is learning to move forward with your eyes glued to the cover ahead, and not on the ground. Your eyes must be searching for a buck all the time!

One of the biggest mistake still-hunters make is not relying on quality optics to help them spot a buck. When bucks are as scarce as fur buyers at a PETA convention, you can't afford to be sloppy. I use my Nikon binoculars to probe the shadows and edge habitat for unusual shapes and out-of-context colors. It is amazing how well a buck can hide, even if he is standing only 50 yards away. Keep in mind that his eyes and ears are a lot better than ours. If he sees or hears you first, you probably won't see him at all.

In the early season, still-hunters do best prowling around food sources, such as acorn hollows, beech ridges, old orchards, and grown-over clear-cuts. Early mornings and late afternoons seem to bring the most action. Keep in mind that your odds are best the first time you sneak and peek through an orchard or along a beech ridge, so wait for conditions to be perfect before you venture ahead.

Don't overlook one of the seasons' first rut signs, however—scrapes and scrape lines! In some areas, there always seems to be a mature doe or two that comes into heat a full month before the peak of the rut. Her presence will attract local bucks in a hurry, and there will be a short flurry of activity. Indeed, the buck Edwards shot twenty minutes into the hunt was probably chasing an early-season hot doe.

Where do you find these scrapes? They often show up where they materialized last season, or they will appear seemingly overnight along cart roads, edges of swamps, creek beds, and plateaus above various waterways. They are quickly abandoned as soon as the early rut is over and may or may not become active again in the pre-rut.

JUST ADD WATER

My favorite technique in the early blackpowder season, however, is using a canoe to get way off the beaten pathway—way off! Indeed, floating downstream into the forest primeval or simply paddling to the far side of lakes and ponds can get you into the back country where bucks die of old age without ever getting a whiff of man.

A canoe can help you reach those bucks that die of old age without ever being disturbed by man.

One autumn a group of us paddled to the inlet of a large Adirondack lake and set up camp inside one of the many lean-tos that are generally available on a first-come first-serve basis. There must have been an early-season hot doe nearby because a scrape line suddenly appeared overnight alongside a small feeder stream. I saw the buck that made those scrapes, a behemoth ten-pointer that eluded me several times. I simply could not see enough of him through the brush to get a clean shot! My plan was to return later during the peak rut, but I never found the time. Mark Eddy told me a non-resident eventually rifled that buck, a 180-class Booner, near the end of the regular season.

A canoe also lets you cover a lot of ground, especially if you elect to float a wilderness river. I like to stop at likely looking areas and still-hunt for an hour or two before continuing on with my journey. This is not only a great way to bag a buck, but also an ingenious method to learn more about that twenty square miles of wilderness you've always wondered about. Of course, that canoe can also transport you and your deer back to civilization—an important consideration if you have a long uphill drag.

What calls work best in the early season? Contact buck grunts, doe grunts, doe bleats, and fawn bleats can all attract deer when used sparingly. Unless you know there is an early-season hot doe nearby, however, avoid tending buck grunts and tending buck grunts coupled with doe-in-heat bleats. The

Put ashore often to still-hunt the edges of swamps and acorn-laden ridges above the water line.

Bucks may be scarce in the deep woods, but you usually have the woods to yourself, which helps make every hunt an adventure.

peak rut hasn't kicked in yet, and these sounds are unnatural at this time of the year.

Rattling can be also effective if you just lightly tickle the antlers. Bucks are sparring at this time of the year and are attracted to the grinding of bone. They will, however, avoid any knock-down drag-out antler clashing. Again, this is simply not a natural activity this early in the deer season.

Finally, here are a few terrain features to pay attention to as you float downstream. I'm always on the lookout for water crossings littered with fresh tracks, as they generally point to hot bedding and feeding locations. The only way to discover what is going on, though, is to backtrack in both directions. Such a task can sometimes lead to a real humdinger of a still-hunting area.

We have found that bucks feed along the edges of waterways and also travel parallel to riverbanks. Thus, brushy points, open meadows, and the edges of adjacent swamps, as well as gentle slopes that lead down to the river, are all good places to check for deer and deer sign. Look, too, for rub lines and early-season scrape lines that delineate stands of soft woods like spruce and hemlock with groves of nut-bearing oak and beech trees. These are always killer still-hunting locations for trophy bucks.

As you can see, an early-season blackpowder hunt can bring you all the excitement of the regular season, minus the crowds and inclement weather. But don't tell too many people. It's a secret!

Index

Air Bobs, 33
Air temperature, 75
Allen, Ken, 222
Arrow drift, 41

Bedding areas
  connecting routs, 113
  doe, 112–113
  hunting strategies, 95–99
  locating, 92–95
  scouting, 68–69, 91–92
Binoculars, 25, 236
Blaze orange, 175–183
Blood-trailing, 147–148, 151–154
  leg wounds, 216–217
  liver hits, 217–218
  marginally hit deer, 213–219
  stomach hits, 218–219
Boone & Crockett buck, 165–172
Boots, 32–33
Bowhunting
  ground zero techniques, 134–138
  in gun season, 180–182
  lessons learned, 155–164
  release, 130–132
  shooting positions, 124–126
  spotting and stalking, 143–144
  in thin cover, 139–144
  timing issues, 129–130
  yardage estimation, 126–129
Bows, 27–29
Bow sights, 30–32

Calling
  See also Sounds
  clear-cuts and, 193–195

early season, 84–85, 238–239
peak rut, 86–88, 113–120
pre-rut, 85–86
rattle bags and boxes, 88–89
safety issues and rattling, 50
while moving, 82–84
Camouflage
  blaze orange and, 175–183
  bow, 28–29
  bowhunting in gun season, 180–182
  techniques, 4–5, 135–136
Canoes, use of, 237–238
Cavaleri, Carmen, 184–185
Clear-cuts
  calling in, 193–195
  hunting in, 184–193
Clothing
  boots, 32–33
  camouflage and blaze orange,
    175–183
  gloves, 224–225
  outerwear, 33–34
  in snow, 179
  3-D, 177
Cloud cover, 77

Deer sign, checking for, 7–10, 14–16
Does
  bedding areas, 112–113
  feeding areas, 110–111
  travel lanes, 111
Drury, Mark, 120

Early season
  around water, 237–238
  calling in, 84–85, 238–239

food sources, 235–236
  strategies, 236–237
Eddy, Mark, 222–223
Edges, 102–104
Equipment
  binoculars, 25, 236
  bows, 27–29
  bow sights, 30–32
  flagging tape, 26
  grunt tubes, 25–26
  quivers, 28
  packs, 34

Feeding sites
  doe, 110–111
  early season, 235–236
  scouting, 66–68
Flagging tape, 26, 147–148

Gloves, 224–225
Ground conditions, 9–10
Grunt tubes, 25–26, 113–120
  See also Calling

Heberlein, Thomas A., 53–54
Hunting locations, scouting
  basic techniques, 5–6, 64–65
  bedding areas, 68–69
  feeding sites, 66–68
  travel routes, 69–70

Idaho, 188–189

Kayser, Jon, 188–189

Leaf drop, 76–77
Leg wounds, 216–217
Liver hits, 217–218

Marginally hit deer, tracking, 213–219
Massett, Jim, 225–226
Miraglia, Allen, 151

New Brunswick, 187–188
Noise. See Sounds
Nolan, Wade, 185–186

Physiological responses
  coping mechanisms, 55–60
  heart rates, 53–55
Pikowicz, Zane, 186–187
Practicing, 221–222

Quivers, 28

Rain, hunting in, 200–201
Range finder, 127
Rattle bags and boxes, 88–89
Rattling, safety issues and, 50
Receivers, keeping from freezing,
  225–226
Release, 130–132
Rifles and shotguns
  practicing, 221–222
  receivers, keeping from freezing,
    225–226
  selecting, 223–224
  shot selection, 228–232
  sighting systems, 222–223
  slings, 226
Rifle season, bowhunting in, 180–182
Rut
  signs, 70–72
  sounds, 48–50
  stage, 9, 81
Rut, peak
  calling during, 86–88, 113–120
  hunting strategies, 108–120
  scrape lines, 106–107
Rut, pre-
  calling during, 85–86
  scrape lines, 105–106

Saskatchewan, 186–187
Scent
  controlling human, 6–7
  myths about, 17–19
Scrape and rub lines, 20–21, 86,
  101–102
  early season, 104–105
  peak rut, 106–107
  pre-rut, 105–106
Shooting position, 22–23
Shot selection, 228–232
Sighting systems, 222–223
Slings, 226

Snow, hunting in, 202–204
Snow cover, 77, 80
Sounds
    See also Calling
    clicking, 117–118
    controlling, 11
    feeding, 45–47
    growling, 119–120
    hoof beats, 47–48
    myths about, 16–17
    rattling, 50
    rutting, 48–50
    snort-wheeze, 118–119
    tending grunts, 116–117
Speed, determining your, 7–10
Stedman, Richard C., 53–54
Stomach hits, 218–219
Storms
    deer behavior in, 80
    hunting in, 202–204
Strickland, Warren, 57–60

Thin cover, hunting in, 139–144
Time of day, 9, 19
Tracking hits, 147–154, 205–212
    marginally hit deer, 213–219
Tracking skills, importance of, 227–228
Travel routes, scouting, 69–70
Trecartin, Jerry, 187–188

Walking, tips for, 11–12
Water, use of canoes, 237–238
Wind, 10, 35
    direction, importance of, 74
    high, 39–41, 196–200
    prevailing, 36–37
    steady, 37–38
    thermals, 38–39
    variable, 42
    velocity, 74–75

Yardage estimation, 126–129